I0119707

Horace Stewart

History of the Worshipful Company of Gold and Silver Wyre-Drawers,

and of the origin and development of the industry which the Company represents

Horace Stewart

History of the Worshipful Company of Gold and Silver Wyre-Drawers,
and of the origin and development of the industry which the Company represents

ISBN/EAN: 9783337285258

Printed in Europe, USA, Canada, Australia, Japan

Cover: Foto ©ninafisch / pixelio.de

More available books at **www.hansebooks.com**

THE MASTER'S BADGE AND CHAIN OF OFFICE.

HISTORY

OF

THE WORSHIPFUL COMPANY

OF

GOLD AND SILVER WYRE-DRAWERS

AND OF

*THE ORIGIN AND DEVELOPMENT OF THE INDUSTRY
WHICH THE COMPANY REPRESENTS.*

COMPILED BY

HORACE STEWART

CITIZEN AND GOLD AND SILVER WYRE-DRAWER (MASTER, 1888).

ILLUSTRATED BY

ESTELLE D'AVIGDOR.

LONDON:

PRINTED FOR THE COMPANY BY

The Leadenhall Prefs, E.C.

1891

THE LEADENHALL PRESS, LONDON, E.C.

(R. 1259)

TO

GABRIEL LINDO, Esq., C.C., F.R.G.S., Master,

AND

DAVID EVANS, Ald., WILLIAM HAYS,

E. F. BREWSTER FULLER, DANIEL WELLBY, F.R.G.S.,

WARDENS OF THE WORSHIPFUL COMPANY

OF

GOLD AND SILVER WYRE-DRAWERS,

THIS BOOK IS MOST RESPECTFULLY DEDICATED

BY THEIR FRIEND AND COLLEAGUE,

THE AUTHOR.

PREFACE.

IN offering this little work for the consideration of all those who are interested in the past history of the Gold and Silver Wyre-Drawers, the Author is painfully conscious of the many defects and shortcomings which manifest themselves herein. Indeed, but for the great interest which, in common with every one of its members, he takes in the welfare and prosperity of the Company, and for the hope that this feeling of interest might be stimulated and extended by the publication of the many curious facts related in the following pages, this book had never seen the light.

As it is, the Author must claim from his critics that kind indulgence which is invariably extended to a maiden effort in the thorny, if enticing, field of literature ; the more so, that it is made by one whose vocation and training is far removed from that of a man of letters.

If then, for once, good intentions may be held to be of some account, and those who sit in judgment upon this history, will consider the bricks and stones of solid fact of which it is constructed, rather than the quality of the mortar and cement which bind them together, the Author may, with some measure of confidence, await the result, and feel that the temerity which has emboldened him to attempt the compiling of these interesting chronicles has not been entirely without justification.

The task, owing to lack of time available, and probably to inexperience in the method of dealing with such work, has been somewhat laborious, but it has been essentially a "labour of love," and one of the most pleasing reminiscences connected therewith will be the recollection of the extreme courtesy, and readiness to assist, which the Author has experienced at the hands of those gentlemen who have charge of the Official Documents and Public Records.

Especially are his grateful thanks due to Mr. Dorset Eccles, of the Department of Printed Books at the British Museum, for the very great trouble and interest taken by him in this little work, and for the valuable information he has so kindly afforded. Also to Mr. S. R. Scargill Bird, of the Public Record Office, for many useful hints and for searches made through the Rolls. And to Mr. Edward Rigg, Chief Clerk at the Royal Mint, who, by kind permission of the Comptroller, Sir Charles Freemantle, C.B., placed the Records of that ancient Institution at the Author's service.

The Town Clerk, Sir John B. Monckton, has likewise very kindly given permission for search to be made through the Records of the Corporation, upon several points of interest relating to the Company ; and much extremely useful advice has been received from Mr. Charles Welch, the courteous librarian to the Corporation of the City of London.

Sir Walter Prideaux, Clerk to the Worshipful Company of Goldsmiths, has also afforded some very valuable information from the Minute Books of that great Company, confirming and supplementing the Mint Records. And Mr. Clark, of Godliman Street, has taken much trouble in putting before the Author his rare collection of Books on Heraldry, from which was obtained the first intimation of the earlier Incorporation of the Company.

To all these gentlemen the Author begs to tender his sincere and grateful acknowledgments of the very great service they have rendered to him, and through him, to the Worshipful Company of Gold and Silver Wyre-Drawers.

A debt of gratitude is likewise due from the Author, to Miss Estelle d'Avigdor, daughter of one of the youngest of the liverymen, who has voluntarily devoted her artistic talent to designing the series of historical and technical illustrations which adorn this work; thereby greatly enhancing its importance, and adding to the interest which, it is hoped, may be taken in the many quaint and remarkable incidents narrated in its various chapters.

SPRINGFIELD,
 HENDON, N. W.
June, 1891.

CONTENTS.

—◆—

CHAPTER VII.

CHAPTER VIII.

CHAPTER IX.

CHAPTER X.

CHAPTER XI.

CHAPTER XII.

CHAPTER XIII.

APPENDIX.

LIST OF PLATES.

LIST OF HEAD AND TAILPIECES ILLUSTRATING THE HISTORY
OF THE WYRE-DRAWERS' COMPANY.

LIST OF AUTHORITIES AND BOOKS OF REFERENCE QUOTED IN THIS HISTORY.

Old Testament : Genesis and Exodus.

"Encyclopædia Britannica."

"National Encyclopædia."

Homer : (Pope's translation of the "Iliad" and "Odysscy.")

"Archæologia," Vols. I., III., IX., XII., XVI., XXIX., XLI., XLII., XLV., XLIX., and L.

"Rolls of Parliament," Vols. II., III., and IV.

"Statutes and Acts."

"House of Commons Journals," Vols. I., II., VIII., XI., XXIV., XXV., and XXVII.

"House of Lords Journals" Vols. III. and XXVI.

"Royal Proclamations." Collection at British Museum.

"Patent Roll." 21 Jac. 1, part 2.

"Calendar of State Papers," (Domestic Series) : Henry VIII., Edward VI. to James I., Charles I., Commonwealth, and Charles II.

Cobbett's "Parliamentary History."

Collier's "History of the British Empire."

"City Repertories," Vols. VIII. and XCV.

"Royal Mint, Records of."

"Goldsmith's Company, Records of."

Edmondson's "Complete Body of Heraldry."

Berry's "Encyclopædia Heraldica."

Burke's "General Armory."

Robson's "British Herald."

Riley's "Memorials of London Life."

"Analytical Index to the Remembrancia."

Rymer's "Fœdera" (Syllabus in English).

Nicholas' "Ordinances of the Privy Council."

Planché's " Cyclopædia of Costume."

Rüding's " Annals of the Coinage."

Beckmann's " History of Inventions."

Yeats's " History of Commerce."

Violet, Thos., " Tracts," published 1653 and 1656; "Appeal to Cæsar," published 1660.

" Historical Books," Library of the Corporation.　" Choice Scraps," Library of the Corporation.

John Waller, Wire-drawer, " Appeal to Nobility and Gentry," published 1755.

" Chambers's Journal."　Article in March Number of 1889.

AARON . HELEN . INNOCENT III . ELIZABETH . CHARLES I. 33TH 11TH HUSSAR

HISTORY OF THE
GOLD AND SILVER WYRE-DRAWERS.

INTRODUCTION.

THE ancient craft which the Gold and Silver Wyre-Drawers Company represents, may be best described by quoting the words used in the preamble of the present Charter of Incorporation, which are as follows :—

" The Trade Art and Mistery of Drawing and
" Flatting of Gold and Silver Wyre, and Makeing
" and Spinning of Gold and Silver Thread and Stuffe within the
" Cities of London and Westminster, the Borrough of Southwark, and
" all other places within Thirty Miles distance from the same."

From the above description it will at once be seen that the industry with which the Company is, and always has been connected, is that of the working and weaving of all those fabrics destined to be used on vestments, and other articles of personal apparel, and for general decorative purposes, in which Gold and Silver Wire and Thread form a component part. The principal of these fabrics are Gold and Silver Lace, Fringes, Bullion-Cords and Tassels, etc.

B

It will also be obvious that, in consequence of its peculiar nature (the trade being so intimately related to all matters connected with dress), this handicraft, during the many centuries (both before and after the incorporation of the Company) in which it has been practised, has experienced many vicissitudes of fortune, owing to the vagaries of that fickle goddess " Fashion."

Working moreover almost entirely in the precious metals, it has found itself, much to the detriment and hindrance of the industry, mixed up with important State questions relating to the supply of Bullion and Coin, and has consequently been the object of many enactments, proclamations, and Acts of Parliament for regulating, checking, and even suppressing the Trade.

In spite of these difficulties and drawbacks, the Gold and Silver Wyre-Drawers have managed to hold their own, and play a very creditable part in the history of the Guilds of the City of London. Sometimes in a very flourishing condition, and employing many thousands of hands, at others, owing to change of fashion, finding themselves in the cold shade of neglect, they have come down to the present day, diminished in numbers, but with their Art in the highest state of perfection, and ready, by the help of all the latest mechanical improvements to avail themselves to the fullest extent of any increased demand, such as the present fashion seems to indicate, for their productions. And if the Gold and Silver Wyre-Drawers' Company cannot carry its history as a corporation so far back into the past as do many of the great City Guilds (as a matter of fact it is one of the youngest of these bodies), it is none the less true that the origin of the Trade, Art, and Mystery with which the Company is identified, is lost in the mists of antiquity; for one has to go back to Ancient Egyptian, Greek, and Roman times, to find the earliest mention of the use of Gold Wire in woven fabrics.

The Arms borne by the Company are thus described by Joseph Edmondson, F.S.A., Mowbray Herald, in his work entitled " The Complete Body of Heraldry."

Gold and Silver Wire-Drawers, (London).

Incorporated 14th June, 21 Jac. I, 1623.

Arms.

Az. on a chevron or, between two coppers in chief of the second, in base two points in saltier ar. a drawing iron between rings (*i.e.* tools used by Wire-drawers) sa.

Crest.

Two arms embowed, vested gu., cuffed ar., holding between their hands, proper, an engrossing block, or.

Supporters.

The dexter, an Indian proper, crowned with an Eastern crown, or., vested round the middle with feathers pendent alternately ar. and gu., holding over his shoulder a bar of silver. The sinister, a man vested proper (called in the grant a Silk Throwster), in his sinister hand a hank of silk ar.

MOTTO.

"Amicitiam trahit Amor."

Some doubt exists as to the exact date of the granting of these Arms. They are, however, found engraved on the Common Seal of the Company presented in 1742, by Nicholas Cunliffe, who became master in the ensuing year. Edmondson, who wrote in 1780, describes them as above, and is confirmed by William Berry, who was for fifteen years Registering Clerk to the College of Arms, in his " Encyclopædia Heraldica," published in 1828.

Sir Bernard Burke, Ulster King at Arms, in his work "General Armory of Great Britain" adopts the same description, which is likewise given in Robson's " British Herald," published in 1830.

Before commencing the thread of this history, it may be as well to explain that, in consequence of the amount of information that has been found available, it has been thought advisable to divide it practically into four parts :—

The first part, dealing with the use of gold wire and thread from the earliest known times down to and including the Tudor period, is treated of in the first three chapters.

The second portion, relating to the chequered career of the "Wierdrawers" under the Stuarts, viz. : during the ninety years immediately preceding their final Incorporation, forms the subject of the three following chapters.

The third part, describing the second Incorporation of the Company, its early struggles, its Parliamentary record, and its history down to the time when a Livery was granted in 1780, comprises the next four chapters.

The last portion, referring to the Livery Grant, followed by a period of decline and fall, and finally by the resuscitation of the Company in 1879, and its restoration to its present prosperous condition, is made up of the three concluding chapters.

The Appendix recites the various Acts of Parliament obtained by the Company, and gives a complete list of the Masters and other Officers of the Company from the date of its Incorporation down to the present time, together with other interesting details.

CHAPTER I.

THE USE OF GOLD WIRE TRACED FROM ANCIENT DOWN TO ANGLO-SAXON TIMES.

Encyclopædia Britannica. T would be an impossible task to trace back the stream of time in order to try to find the actual birthplace of the practice of using Gold Wire or Thread in articles of apparel, but it is known that the ancient Egyptians were familiar with this work, and through whom the Hebrews, in due course, became acquainted with it. Many circum-Genesis xxxvii. 25. Exodus xxx. (National Encyclopædia.) stances, however, point to the conclusion that the Art originated in India, whence the Egyptians were in the habit of obtaining the various spices and perfumes (especially Cassia and Cinnamon) which they used so largely, and that by means of this intercourse between the two countries, the Art was passed on. Be this as it may, one has to go back through the history of the world for no less than three thousand three hundred years, viz. to B.C. 1491, in order to find the first mention of the use of Gold Wire in a woven fabric.

Exodus xxxix. 2, 3. The passage occurs in the description of the Ephod made for Aaron, and is as follows :—

"And he made the Ephod of Gold, blue, and purple, and scarlet, "and fine twined linen. And they did beat the Gold into thin plates, "and cut it into wires, to work it in the blue, and in the purple, and in "the scarlet, and in the fine linen, with cunning work."

That the Art of thinning down and working (or weaving) the precious metals into articles of personal apparel was known to the ancients, is also proved by the frequent allusions made by Homer, both in the "Iliad" and the "Odyssey," to inwoven and embroidered golden textiles.

Fair Helen is found by Iris, at Troy, seated at her loom, and weaving her own sad story into the golden web, whilst aged Priam's treasure-chambers were stored with gold-embroidered robes. Thus, Hector bids his mother Hecuba

> ". . . Take
> "The largest mantle your full wardrobes hold.
> " Most prized for art, and laboured o'er with gold.
> " To spread before Minerva's honoured knees."

Again, when Priam goes forth to ransom from dread Achilles the body of Hector, he takes "from forth his opened stores" amongst other treasures—

> " Twelve fair veils, and garments stiff with gold."

And when the bones of Hector were removed from the funeral pyre and placed in a golden vase,

> " The golden vase in purple palls they roll'd
> " Of softest texture, and inwrought with gold."

In the palace of Ulysses, at Ithaca, Penelope's suitors are described as garbed " with purple robes inwrought and stiff with gold."

And when Telemachus visits Menelaüs at Sparta, his couch, by beauteous Helen's command, is thus prepared—

> " And o'er soft palls of purple grain unfold,
> " Rich tapestry, stiff with inwoven gold."

Ulysses, before making himself known to Penelope, thus, at her command, delineates her warlike lord—

> ". . . In ample mode
> " A robe of military purple flow'd
> " O'er all his frame ; illustrious on his breast
> " The double clasping gold the King confessed.

"In the rich woof a hound mosaic drawn,
"Bore on full stretch and seized a dappled fawn,
"Deep in the neck his fangs indent their hold,
"They pant and struggle in the moving gold.
"Fine as a filmy web beneath it shone
"A vest that dazzled like a cloudless sun."

And, lastly, Penelope's famous web is thus described—

". . . Before us lay
"The mingled web, whose gold and silver ray
"Displayed the radiance of the night and day."

Encyclopædia Britannica (Textiles and Embroidery). Herodotus likewise bears witness that this Art was known to the Ancient Egyptians; instancing—A Pallium sent by King Amasis to the Spartans, which contained no less than three hundred and sixty threads—the figures woven on this being partly of cotton and partly of gold thread.

Beckmann's History of Inventions (Wire-drawing). In the writings of Pliny several references are made to this kind of work; showing that it was well known to and used by the Romans. One example is that of the mantle taken by Dionysius from the statue of Jupiter; another the tunic of Heliogabalus; they also gave the name of "Attalica" to a costly Cloth of Gold belonging to the Art **Encyclopædia Britannica.** treasures of Attalus II., of Pergamum. Pliny, however, speaks of this cloth of Attalus as being embroidered with the needle, and draws a clear distinction between this and the woven work, which was of earlier date. Beckmann states that gold was interwoven with linen during the third century, and some idea of the richness of the fabrics which were made at this period, may be gathered from the fact that when the grave of the wife of the Emperor Honorius was discovered at Rome, about the year 1544, thirty-six pounds of Gold Wire was procured from the mouldering dress which contained the body. Beckmann also refers to a statement by Pliny, that dresses both at that time and formerly were woven or knit entirely of Gold Threads.

From this time onwards, the sister Arts of weaving and embroidering with Gold Wire appear to have been practised side by side, for frequent mention is made of examples of both kinds of work belonging to the Anglo-Saxon period.

Beckmann thus describes another mode of using Gold and Silver

Wire. The work was called "Filigrane" or "Ouvrage de Filigrane;" and was made from Fine Gold and Silver Wire, often curled and twisted in a serpentine form, and sometimes plaited. The Art is spoken of as being of great antiquity, and as having been brought to Europe from the East. The earliest known example consists of a Cross, ornamented with filigrane work which was made by St. Eloy, who died A.D. 665. This cross was lately preserved in an Abbey at Paris.

The beautiful "Opus Anglicum," which was produced at the time of the Anglo-Saxons, affords indubitable evidence of the very early date at which the Art of embroidering with Gold Thread was practised in England, for it is on record that so far back as the seventh century, a Stole and Maniple, embroidered with Gold, were presented to St. Cuthbert by St. Ethelreda, Queen, and first Abbess of Ely; and about one hundred years later, viz. A.D. 800, Deubart, Bishop of Durham, granted the lease of a farm of two hundred acres for life to the Embroideress Eanswitha, for the charge of scouring, repairing, and renewing the embroidered vestments of the Priests. A fine example of Early English embroidered work, known as "the Sion Monastery Cope," is preserved in the collection at South Kensington. *Encyclopædia Britannica (Embroidery).*

When, during the reign of Charles I., the reputed tomb of William Rufus was opened at Winchester, certain reliques of Cloth of Gold, which were supposed to have formed part of the Royal vestments, were found: considerable doubt has, however, arisen as to whether this tomb was really that of the second Norman king, and in a paper on the subject read before the Society of Antiquaries in 1869, by Rev. James Gerald Joyce, it was stated that these fragments of Gold Lace, which are beautifully illustrated on Plate XVII. of the 42nd volume of the "Archæologia," were compared with some lent by Mr. Franks, and were pronounced to be of Saxon origin and date; the conclusion was therefore arrived at, that these remains, which had been so wantonly disturbed by the Roundhead soldiers, were those of some Anglo-Saxon prince or warrior. *Archæologia, vols. iii. and xlii.*

Another fragment of Gold Lace has been discovered in a Scandinavian barrow at Wareham, in Dorset; the remains of a distinct lozenge pattern being still traceable, similar to that found on the *Cyclopædia of Costume, by J. Robinson Planché (Somerset Herald).*

Archæologia, vol. ix., Plate viii.

borders of Anglo-Saxon and Danish dresses of the tenth and eleventh centuries. And in a paper read before the Society of Antiquaries, by Ph. Rashleigh, Esq., in 1788, giving an account of certain antiquities found at St. Austells, in Cornwall, in 1774, mention is made, and an illustration given of a plaited Silver Wire cord, discovered with a lot of coins, one of which being of Burgred, last King of Mercia (A.D. 874).

CHAPTER II.

HAT the excellence of the English work was well maintained, is proved by the following anecdote related by Matthew of Paris :—

"About this time (1246) the Lord Pope "(Innocent IV.), having observed that the ecclesi- "astical ornaments of some Englishmen, such as "choristers' copes, and mitres, were embroidered in "gold thread after a very desirable fashion, asked where these works "were made, and received in answer, 'in England.'

"'Then,' said the Pope, 'England is surely a garden of delight for "us. It is truly a never-failing spring, and there where many things "abound much may be extorted.'

"Accordingly, the same Lord Pope sent sacred and sealed briefs to "nearly all the Abbots of the Cistercian order established in England, "requesting them to have forthwith forwarded to him these em- "broideries in Gold, which he preferred to all others, and with which "he wished to adorn his chasuble and choral cope, as if these objects "cost them nothing."

The more extended use that the nobles were beginning to make

Encyclopædia Britannica.

of these costly manufactures is shown by the following curious document :—

Riley's
Memorials of
London Life.

"28th October, 1304.

"Thomas Guy Dichon of Lucca to Alison Darcy.

"Quit claim of all interest in a piece of cloth embroidered with "Gold and Silk, which she is now preparing—eight ells in length, and "six ells in breadth—in consideration of 300 marks Sterling received "from Henry de Lacy—Earl of Lincoln, and Sir John de Sandale.

"Given before the Mayor of London and other Aldermen."

Archæologia,
vol. iii.

In another paper read before the Society of Antiquaries, it is stated that when the tomb of Edward I., who died A.D. 1307, was opened in 1774, the body of the King was found wrapped in a mantle of Cloth of Gold. The late Dean Stanley, in yet another most interesting paper

Archæologia,
vol. xlv.

on the examination of the Tombs of Richard II. and Henry III., in Westminster Abbey, read by him before the same Society in 1873, mentions that the coffin of Henry III., was found to be completely covered, back, front, ends, and top, with crimson Cloth of Gold, the warp being composed of Gold Threads similar to that now used by Arras weavers, the weft being only of crimson silk. The design is described as a Diaper pattern of great beauty, consisting of striped stars and eight foils alternately. A woodcut of this pattern is given in the paper.

Vol. ii. pp.
278–282.

The Rolls of Parliament show that in 1364, 37 Edward III., a Sumptuary Law was passed referring to the wearing of Gold-embroidered vestments ; it was, however, during the following reign that a great impetus was given to the demand for these articles of apparel.

Richard the Second, whose ruling passion was the love of display, seems to have greatly encouraged the workers and traders in Gold

Rolls of Parliament, vol.
ii. p. 47.

and Silver Thread ; for in the second year of his reign, permission was given to foreign merchants to reside in England, and trade in Gold and Silver Wire (" Fil d'or et d'argent ").

Collier's History of the
British Empire.

Frequent mention is made of the extravagant richness of the King's dress, which is described as being " stiff with Gold and Gems," and in Ashmole's " History of the Order of the Garter " it is stated that, " In

Archæologia,
vol. xxix.

"the reign of King Richard II. the little garters with which the robes "of the Sovereign and Knights Commanders were adorned, were "embroidered in Cyprus Gold." The Queen's dress is also described Archæologia, vol. xxix. as being embroidered with branches of Rosemary and Broom in Cyprus Gold and Silk.

The following references likewise show the general use that was being made at this time of Cloth of Gold for Royal and Ecclesiastical purposes.

Thus, in 1390–91, 14 Richard II., Benderell de Beek, "worker in Nicholas's Ordinances of the Privy Council. Cloth of Gold," petitioned the King for payment of arrears of wages due to him, which was granted.

And when, in September, 1399, the two Houses of Parliament met Collier's History. in Westminster Hall on the occasion of the deposition of the King, the empty throne was covered with Cloth of Gold.

The inventories of St. Paul's Cathedral mention that " 15 pieces of Archæologia, vol. l. "Gold Cloth of Rakemask" were divided amongst the Dean and four of the Canons in the year 1404.

The frequent allusions to Gold-embroidered robes during the next century show that the demand for this work was steadily increasing, and to such an extent as to necessitate the regulation of the trade, and of those working in it. Before, however, dealing with these allusions to the growth of the taste in this country for such costly articles of apparel, it may be as well to briefly trace the progress of this luxurious Art on the Continent of Europe down to the time now under consideration.

Many circumstances point to the conclusion that the Art of weaving Encyclopædia Britannica, vol. x. pp. 373, 374. and embroidering with Gold and Silver originated in India, and thence travelled westward from one great city to another, until Constantinople, and in due course, Venice, became famous centres of these much-prized manufactures; for in the Oriental circles, whence the knowledge of these fabrics is supposed to have first spread, the passion for such costly garments is still most strongly prevalent.

Venice for several centuries maintained her pre-eminence in the Cyclopædia of Costume, by J. Robinson Planché. manufacture of those fabrics and embroideries of Gold and Silver for which she was so justly celebrated, frequent allusions to them being made in Inventories, Wills, and Wardrobe lists of the sixteenth century.

In the Oriental, Sicilian, and early Italian stuffs, Gold Thread was Encyclopædia Britannica. used in a very lavish and effective way.

The method of working or preparing it was as follows : Fine

vellum skins were thickly gilded with gold leaf, the vellum was then cut into very thin strips and wound round a thread of silk or hemp so closely as to look like a solid gold wire.

From Venice the taste for these beautiful fabrics rapidly spread over Europe, notably into Germany, where the Towns of Nüremburg and Augsburg soon became centres for the manufacture of the Wire, which, however, down to the mediæval times, with the exception of the Venetian and Italian method just described, continued to be made after the manner explained in the Pentateuch.

To these two ancient German towns, where the term "Wire-drawer" appears to have originated, belongs the credit of having been the first to produce the Wire by a more mechanical process than that hitherto adopted. As already stated, the earliest method of making Wire consisted in hammering the metal into thin plates, and then cutting it into narrow strips ; and whilst Wire was made in this way by hand, the workmen of Nüremberg, by whom it was manufactured, were styled "Wire-smiths ;" but, according to Beckmann, an ingenious machine for drawing the Wire, and impelled by water, was constructed in this Town about the middle of the fourteenth century by a person named Rudolf or Ludolf, who kept the invention secret for some time, and realized much money by the use of it.

Hence the origin of the term "Wire-drawer," which occurs for the first time in 1351, and again in 1360, in the histories of Nüremberg and of Augsburg respectively. Beckmann mentions that Conrade Celtes, writing in the year 1491, confirmed the previous information as to the place and date of the invention of Wire-drawing.

Owing to their greater ductility, and to the extensive demand for them in this form, it is probable that the precious metals were the first to be drawn into Wire, and that for a short time this process was done by hand.

Reverting to the progress of the trade in England, Gold and Silver Stuffs are first mentioned in connection with the Guilds of London, in 1423, when "The wise and worthie Communes of London, and the "Wardens of Brauderie in the said Citie of London" petitioned the "King against deceit and default in the work of divers persons occupy-"ing the craft of Embroidery."

Marginal notes:

Encyclopædia Britannica.

Beckmann.

Rolls of Parliament, 2 Henry VI. cap. x. vol. iv. p. 255.

This petition led to the following Act being passed :—

It is ordained and assented, "That all the work and stuff of Stat. folio, p.
221. "Embroidery of Gold or of Silver of Cipre (Cyprus) or of Gold of "Luk (Lucca) mixed with Spanish Laton (supposed to be an alloy of "Copper), and exposed for sale in deceit of the Kings liege subjects "shall be forfeited to the King, or to the Lords and others having "Franchises of such forfeitures, in whose Franchise such work shall be "found.

"And this ordinance shall endure until the Parliament next to "come."

About this date an account, accompanied by a petition asking for Archæologia,
vol. xvi. payment of the same, was presented to the King by a merchant, who had supplied vestments, made of Gold of Cyprus, to the order of the Bishop of St. David, for the Royal College of Our Lady of Eton, and for the College of St. Nicholas of Cambridge. And in the same year an Nicholas's
Ordinances of
the Privy
Council, 28
Jan., 1424. Order of the Privy Council was made for the sum of £24 to be paid by the King's gift to James, King of Scotland, against his marriage, for a silk Cloth of Gold.

In 1461, 3 Edward IV., the Court of Common Council appears to House of
Commons
Journals,
vol. i. p. 536. have bestowed some attention upon the Wire-drawers, for it was stated by the Recorder, when giving evidence before the House of Commons in 1620, in the celebrated case of Sir G. Mompesson and others, that in this year, viz. 1461, "An Act of Common Council was passed respecting 'Gold-drawers.'" This Act, however, cannot be traced, although, by the courtesy of the town clerk, Sir John Monckton, search has been made through the City records, and, in a paper read before the Society of Antiquaries by Samuel Rawson Gardiner, Esq., in 1867, on the Archæologia,
vol. xli. subject of certain letters of Lord Bacon's, addressed to King Christian IV. of Denmark, and in which the Mompesson matter is fully gone into, reference is made to this action of the Court of Common Council as being simply the consideration of the case of certain Foreigners in London who were Gold Wire-drawers.

The search for this Act has, however, brought to light a very interesting point in connection with the Iron Wire Drawers, whose industry, according to one authority, was not supposed to have been established in England until nearly one hundred years later, viz. in

Yeats' History of Commerce. 1565, when Christopher Schutz and Daniel Houghsetter were said to have been the first to introduce the art of Wire-drawing into England, under the auspices of Queen Elizabeth ; the point being the discovery of a note of " the petition of the Wyre-drawers, and Chape-makers that City Repertories No. 8, fo. 215 B, 15 Oct. 19 Edward IV. " they may be made one Company, and called Wyre-mongers."

There is no note of any resolution of the Court on the matter.

In another paper read before the Society of Antiquaries by the Archæologia, vol. I. Rev. Dr. Miller, Dean of Exeter, entitled, " Observations on the Wardrobe Accounts for 1483," frequent mention is made of the use of Cloth of Gold of various kinds and colours, on the occasion of the King's (Richard III.) coronation.

The short reign which now began was too brief and troubled for any chronicles of interest to have been handed down relating to this History, and with the advent of the Tudors begins a fresh period, which may be best dealt with in another chapter, the present one closing with a reference to a magnificent specimen of a gold cope, of fifteenth century work, still preserved at Westminster Abbey.

CHAPTER III.

BEFORE treating of the fashions which prevailed during this period. it may be worth while to glance briefly at the progress which these industries were making on the Continent, notably in Germany, although, as will have been seen by the frequent references in the foregoing pages to Cyprus Gold, Gold of Venice, of Lucca, of Florence, and of Genoa, the Italian fabrics had long maintained the exclusive possession of the English Market.

According to Beckmann, much important information, taken from original papers, has been published by Dr. Hirsching, of Erlangen, respecting the Wire-drawing industry at Nüremberg and Augsburg. This authority states that Andrew Schultz, in 1545, brought to Augsburg the Art of drawing very fine Gold and Silver Wire as he had learnt it in Italy; and that Gabriel Marteningi and his son Vincent were invited from Italy to teach the Art of making Gold Fringe.

George Gyer, who learnt under them, was the first person to introduce the process of the flatting of Wire at Augsburg, and in the year 1570 a Frenchman, named Anthony Fournier, brought to Nüremberg the Art of drawing Wire exceedingly fine.

Beckmann.
(Dr. Hirsch-ing.)

C

Beckmann.
Dr. Hirsching.
In 1592 Frederick Hagelscheimer, of Nüremberg, began to prepare Fine Gold and Silver Wire, such as could be used for spinning round silk and for weaving; and which had previously only been manufactured in France and Italy.

Ibid.
Hagelscheimer, or Held (as he was sometimes called), received an exclusive Patent for his work, for fifteen years; which Patent was, in 1617, continued for fifteen years longer, and was subsequently several times renewed; finally, by the advice of the Imperial Council, these Patents were converted into a fief to the heirs male of the family.

Beckmann states that the flatting mills used for flatting the wire, preparatory to spinning, first came from Milan; but that now, viz. middle of the nineteenth century, they are supplied from Neuchâtel. (At the present time they are manufactured by Herr Krupp.) He also mentions the exclusive patents granted by the Emperor and the Imperial Council at Nüremberg, and refers to the fine work successfully carried on in France and Italy, and the many improvements brought thence into Germany.

Beckmann, quoting from Anderson's " History of Commerce" and "Husbandry and Trade Improved," adds that the first wire making (? iron) in England was established at Esher or Sheen by J. Momma and D. Demetrius, and that the first flatting mill was established at Sheen (near Richmond) by a Dutchman in 1663. This locality appears to have been a favourite spot for this industry, for the City Records state that the manufacture of Copper and Brass Wire was commenced in this country at Sheen, by two foreigners, about the year 1649.

Taking up the thread of the story at the commencement of the Tudor period, the same City Guild is again seen to be concerned in the affairs of this Trade; for in 1489, the Wardens and Fellowship of Broderers 4 Henry VII.
cap. 22. obtained an Act of Parliament against the deceitful weight and working of Gold of Venice, Florence, and Jeane (Genoa) and the untrue packing thereof.

This Act ordained that " No person should sell for a pound weight "of such Gold, less than twelve ounces, nor Gold packed differently "from the outward show thereof, viz.:—Not wrought in greatness of "thread, in color, according to the outward show."

In some curious books belonging to the Library of the Corporation

of the City of London, mention is made in the Privy Purse expenses of Historical Books, vol. ii.
Elizabeth of York, of the purchase of both flat and round gold from
" the Queen's Brawderer," in 1502.

Comparatively few references to the use of Gold and Silver in apparel
occur however during the reign of Henry VII. ; but this may well be
attributed to the notorious avarice of the King, which, leading him to
avoid extravagance in display in his own person, also discouraged any
similar luxuriousness on the part of his subjects.

With the accession of Henry VIII. a very different state of things Collier's History.
was inaugurated. As often happens, the miser father had a spendthrift
son. Encouraged by the Earl of Surrey, the young King plunged into
a whirl of costly pleasures ; tournaments, dances, pageants, revels
followed in quick succession, and the nation, ground down by the avarice
of the late king, gladly welcomed to the throne a prince seemingly so
gallant and generous.

As a natural result of so much festivity and rejoicing, the demand
for the costly personal adornments of which this history treats, at once
revived, and the chronicles of this reign are full of references to the
lavish use that was made of these beautiful fabrics.

In a paper on the Wardrobe Accounts of Henry VIII. read before Archæologia, vol. ix.
the Society of Antiquaries, frequent mention is made of the use of
" Venice Gold," and in " Gibson's account of the Revels," similar Cal. of State Papers (Domestic and Foreign,) 1509–1514.
references often occur. Large sums of money were continually being
paid by Henry to Italian Merchants, for Cloth of Gold and other such
wares ; in some instances as much as £500 and £600 being expended
with one man at a time.

About this date the first allusion is made to the use of "Spangles," Archæologia, vol. xlix.
which, together with " flat Gold beaten into wire, damask Gold, and
Cloth of Gold," were employed in the adornment of the King's
Pavilion.

In 1511, a license was granted to Francis de Barde, Merchant, of Cal. of State Papers.
Florence, to import Cloth of Silk and Gold ; and in 1513, a similar
license was given to Laurence Bonvixi, Merchant, of Lucca, and to Rolls of Parliament,
William Bulla, Mercer, of London ; whilst in 1512, an Act was passed 4 Hen. VIII. cap. 6.
authorizing the sealing of Cloth of Gold and Silver.

Magnificent dresses of Cloth of Gold and Damask Gold were worn

Cal. of State
Papers
at the reception of the French Ambassadors in London in 1518, and many of the nobles are described as having greatly impoverished themselves by their lavish expenditure on this occasion. A similar display of extravagant luxury was made on the return visit of the English to Paris.

Ibid.
The use of Cloth of Gold upon the tents and pavilions, and in the splendid dresses of the great personages who assisted at the famous meeting between Henry VIII. and Francis I. on the field situated between the Towns of Guisnes and Ardres, caused that spot to be named " Le Camp du Drap d'Or." Much Venice Gold is stated to have been used in making the flowers and fruit of the artificial " Tree of Honour" which supported the shields of the Challengers at the Tournament on this occasion.

Henry's dress was at all times very rich, and frequent descriptions of his garments occur in old manuscripts. His hose is thus MSS. Har-
leian, No.
1419.
Planché. described.

" One pair (of hose) of purple silk and Venice Gold, woven like a " caul, etc., etc."

And the dress in which he met Ann of Cleves is particularized as follows :—

Planché.
" A coat of velvet, made like a frock, embroidered all over with "flatted gold of damask, with small lace mixed between of the same "gold, and other laces of the same going transversewise."

Henry also appears to have bestowed great attention upon the dress of his favourites, the wardrobe accounts making frequent references to purchases for the robes of these ladies. The following items will serve as examples :—

Historical
Books, vol.
ii.
" 1536-7. Itm̄ payed to the Golde-drawer for Pypes and Pyrles for a gown to my lade Grace.   vijlixvij s̄.

" 1540. Itm̄ payed for one lb. đ. of Golde for embrawdring of a nȳght gowne.

Privy Purse of
Queen Mary
(? Princess).
" 1544. Itm̄ payed to Me Clarentieulx for ij vnce of Wyre Golde."

The State Papers also mention the delight of Henry's sister Margaret, Queen of Scotland, at seeing the magnificent garments of Cloth of Gold, etc., sent to her by her brother. She is said to have left a sick bed on purpose to view them.

One or two short references to Venice Gold and Silver, etc., will now suffice to carry on the history down to the reign of Elizabeth.

Thus in 1553 a warrant, under sign manual, was issued to the Receiver General to pay William Ibgrave, Embroiderer, his account for work done by him for the late King Edward VI., as follows :— _{Cal. of State Papers.}

Embroidering Jerkin with Venice Silver	... ...	4	0	0
Doublet of the same...	... ...	3	0	0
Pair of Hose	... ...	2	15	0
Silver used in above @ £4 per lb. ...	... ...	12	0	0
20 ounces of Damask Silver @ 6/8 per oz.	... ...	6	13	4
		£28	8	4

And in the accounts for the Funeral of this Prince, similar references occur. Viz. :— _{Archæologia, vol. xii.}

Cloth of Gold tissued with Gold and Silver, 20 yds. qr. di.
To Lawrence Ball for 6 lbs. 11 oz. of Fringe of Venice Gold @ 7/4
   per oz.... ... ... 30 12 4
To the same, for the like goods, 9 lbs. 10 oz. 43 10 10

Passement Lace of Gold and Silver is mentioned in a sumptuary law of Queen Mary. _{Planché's Cyclopædia of Costume.}

"Guipure" or "Parchment" was another name given to a variety of Gold and Silver Lace, and is alluded to in an inventory of the clothes of Mary Queen of Scots, taken in 1561 as "Quimpeures d'Argent," "Geynpeurs d'Or," etc. ; and in a list of the Laces belonging to Queen Elizabeth, preserved in the manuscripts of the British Museum, there is an item as follows :— _{Ibid.}

"Parchement Lace of Watchett and Silver at 7ˢ 3ᵈ the ounce." _{Ibid.}

Having regard to the notorious weakness of Queen Elizabeth for costly articles of apparel, it is at first sight somewhat surprising that, except in the Wardrobe Accounts, so few references to garments trimmed or embroidered with Gold Lace, etc., are to be found in the records of her reign ; but it is probable that, by this time, the use of these fabrics had become so general, and consequently so well-known, that the documents referring to them were no longer deemed worthy of preservation among the State Papers, which at this period dealt with matters of far greater importance.

Collier's History.

There can, however, be little doubt that amongst the three thousand dresses found in her wardrobe after the Queen's death, many were embellished with adornments of Gold and Silver. Indeed, the Tudor Exhibition, recently held in London, furnished a number of examples of this work; notably one consisting of a very handsome gold-embroidered dress, which once belonged to the Virgin Queen, and in the collection of Portraits then brought together, many illustrations were afforded of the use of these fabrics in those days.

Another curious relic of this period, and possessing great interest for Gold and Silver Wyre-Drawers, is " the City Purse," which forms part of the Regalia of the City of London, and is justly considered to be a fine specimen of embroidery in Gold Wire.

Yeats' History of Commerce.

It was during this reign, viz. in 1565, that the Art of Wire-drawing was (as previously stated) introduced into England by Christopher Schutz (probably some relation of Andrew Schütz or Schültz, who in 1545 brought to Augsburg from Italy the art of drawing very fine Gold and Silver Wire or Thread) and Daniel Houghsetter; and that the industry soon became established here, is proved by the evidence given by Mary Forest and others in 1620, before the Commissioners dealing with the matter of Sir G.

Archæologia, vol. xli.

Mompesson; this woman stating that in 38° Elizabeth, viz. A.D. 1596, being then ten years old, she was put apprentice to a Frenchman named John (Jean) Rosineall, then living in London, who made Thread, and taught her and others.

Yeats also states that towards the close of the sixteenth century, Gold and Silver Wire began to be drawn fine enough for weaving and spinning round silken thread.

It was likewise during this reign that the first symptoms of the evil system of monopolies and patents began to show themselves, for

Cal. of State Papers (Domestic Series), vol. i.

in August, 1568, three Citizens of London offered to increase Her Majesty's Customs by £1000 a Year, if they had a grant of the survey of Silks, Venice Gold and Silver, and other costly commodities imported; and in the year 1600 a Patent was granted to Lord

Ibid, vol. v.

Thomas Howard for Venice Gold and Silver.

A State Paper, bearing date 1602, mentions that the abatement during the previous ten years of the Customs on Silks and Venice Gold amounted to £58,715.

The Story now passes on into the next period of English History, where the fortunes of the Gold and Silver Wyre-Drawers are seen to reach their culminating point of interest.

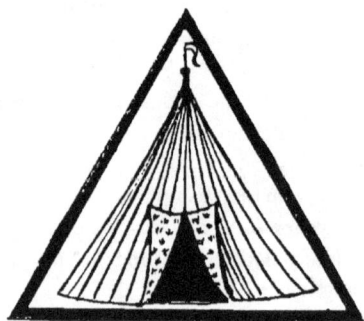

Drawbench.

CHAPTER IV.

LTHOUGH, as will have been seen from the instances referred to in the previous chapters, the use of Gold and Silver Wire for the purposes of Embroidery had been known and practised in England since Anglo-Saxon times, the first really serious attempt to introduce and establish the manufacture in this country of Gold and Silver Thread and the working of it into Lace, appears to have been made about the commencement of the Stuart period, and the story of this (at first) unlucky industry, the vicissitudes of fortune which it experienced, and its chequered career, form a subject of most engrossing interest.

It was the unhappy fate of the Gold and Silver Wyre-Drawers of that time to be the victims of greater and more important interests than their own, and they consequently became the shuttlecock between the King, Parliament, and the Monopolists to whom Patents had been granted.

It was also their misfortune that the exercise of their trade involved the consumption of a large amount of Bullion, then a question of paramount importance to the country, in consequence of the scarcity of the supply of precious metals, and the diminution of the coinage arising therefrom ; and so serious did this question become, that several Royal Proclamations were made, prohibiting the manufacture of Gold and Silver Thread, and restricting the use of Gold Folliat (Gold leaf) in buildings, ceilings, carriages, etc.   And finally, the gross abuses, extortions, and malpractices committed by those persons to whom monopolies or letters patent had been granted, aroused such a storm of indignation, that the attention of Parliament was drawn to the matter ; both Houses were engaged for a considerable time in discussing the question, which had been voted a grievance, and the whole system was condemned and ordered to be done away with.

Feb. 4, 16½, in Library of British Museum (quoted in the Mint Records, Book I, p. 45).

The earliest mention of the Industry during this period occurs in 160⅘, when, " in order to prevent the waste of the more precious " metals, an exclusive Patent for the making of Gold and Silver Thread "was granted to Roger Pennell and Richard Grimstone for sixteen "years from January 13th of this year;" and by a Royal Proclamation " made on the 2nd of February then ensuing, " All persons were for-" bidden to buy or sell any such thread not sealed by the Patentees on "pain of fine and corporal punishment."

Rüding's Annals of the Coinage, p. 364.

In the Collection belonging to the Privy Council (vide Rüding).

The authorities appear, however, to differ with regard to this record ; for, according to the State Papers, the Patent was granted September 27, 1604,* to Dike Fowle and Dorrington, for twenty-one years, and the grant made to Pennell and Grimstone was that of a lease of the *Customs* on Gold and Silver Thread, the Proclamation of February 2nd being described as confirming this privilege.

Cal. of State Papers (Domestic Series).

The following curious letter is also found : " Viscount Fenton to Salisbury.   Bradshaw is willing to refer his interest in the Patent for Gold and Silver Thread to Salisbury."

The next allusion to this trade appears from the Records of the City of London to have been made in 1611, when the Silkmen of the City petitioned the King to be incorporated as a company.

The matter was referred by the Commissioners of Suits to the Lord Mayor and Court of Aldermen, who reported unfavourably to the proposal, stating that—

Analytical Index to the Remembrancia.

" With regard to the abuses complained of, viz. falsity in working,

---

* This date is evidently an error. It should be 1614, the paper being a docket relating to the second Patent granted Jan. 10, 1616.

"in dyeing, and in weighing of silk and gold and silver thread, they
"were otherwise remedied, and in a better manner than they could be
"by this Company.

" For falsity in working, the Weavers' charter became operative.

" As regarded dyeing, an Act of Common Council was ordained.

" And for falsity in weight, the Statutes of the Realm were
"excellent."

Cal. of State
Papers
(Domestic
Series).

In the same year, a Frenchwoman (Madame Furatta) was brought
over from France to give lessons in the art of working up Gold and
Silver Thread, and under the patronage of the Countess of Bedford,
five persons, named Dike, Fowle, Hum, Phipps, and Dade applied
successfully for a Patent, which was granted May 21, 1611.

Confession of
Sir Henry
Yelverton,
A.D. 1620,
H.C.J., vol. i.
p. 526.

Attempts having been made to infringe this Patent, Sir Henry
Montague, Recorder of London, imprisoned certain offenders, and took
away their tools.

This (? Patent) being opposed, produced authority to the Earl of
Suffolk, and Sir Thomas Lake, etc.

Sir Henry
Yelverton's
Confessions,
Calendar of
State Papers,
and Analytical
Index to the
Remembran-
cia.

In 1616 the old Patent was surrendered, and a new one, to last for
twenty-one years, was at once, viz. January 10, 1616, granted to Fowle,
Dike, and Dorrington, who agreed to pay to the King a rent equal to
the sum obtained from the duty upon importation.

Analytical
Index to the
Remembran-
cia.

Great resistance was raised by the Goldsmiths to this Patent, who,
through the Lord Mayor and Court of Aldermen, petitioned the Privy
Council, complaining

" That the Patentees were unable to do their work without the aid
"of the Goldsmith, although by sinister practices, such as working on
"the poverty of one or two poor artsmen of that Company, they had
"obtained a superficial insight into the mode of working. And that
"the new Patent included the Drawing Milning (? Milling) and Flatting
"of Gold and Silver Thread after the manner practised by the
"Petitioners ; and by which they sought to prohibit all others from
"practising such work ; and furthermore that they (the Patentees) had
"procured the imprisonment of one Moore, a Wyre-drawer, for using
"his trade."

The Court of Aldermen thought fit to recommend the Petition to
the Council, and requested them to hear the Petitioners against the

Patent, and in the meantime to stay the same, and release Moore from prison.

The story is now best continued in the words of Sir Henry Yelver- H. C. J., vol. ton's "ingenuous information" given when examined at the Tower in i. p. 536 1620.

"That upon this Patent Sir Edward Villiers became a partner, " put in a stock, and solicited him (Sir H. Yelverton) then Solicitor- (or " Attorney-) General. That Sir H. Y. upon the offering disliked the " Patent as being a Monopoly, therefore devised the course should be " by Indenture between the King and them, whereby they should be " but Agents, and whereby, if found inconvenient the King might easily " put it down."

"That 16° Jac. 1 (viz. 1618) these indentures accordingly passed " upon a Petition to the King by Sir Edward Villiers, in the name of " Fowle and Dike. That the King's care was exceedingly great " before he made his grant. He made reference to the new Lord " Chancellor, Treasurer, and Sir Henry Yelverton. They certified the " course good if well used ; and approved the said device of Sir H. " Yelverton."

This arrangement was duly notified by Royal Proclamation made Cal. of State on March 22, 16$\frac{18}{19}$, wherein the King states that, " in order to pre- Ruding's l'apers, " vent abuses by the counterfeiting of Gold and Silver Thread, he Coinage, and " had caused the whole work to be taken into his possession rather Index to the " than leave it to the disposal and power of private men. And Fowle cia. " was made the crown Agent." Annals of the Analytical Remembran-

In April a commission was given to the Lord Chancellor and others Cal. of State to inquire into the importation of Gold and Silver Thread, which was l'apers. again forbidden, and likewise the making of any engine for drawing of Gold and Silver Thread. And on the 10th of October of the following Ibid. year another Proclamation was issued, reaffirming the previous one.

This, however, led to serious steps being taken to thwart the Analytical Patent. In 1619 several silk mercers were committed to the Fleet ; Remembran-when four Aldermen offered to stand bail for them for £100,000. cia. The King, therefore, set them at liberty. Index to the

In the same year two more licenses were granted by the King, one Cal. of State to W. Bennett and others to make and sell Gold and Silver Thread for l'apers.

three years; and the other on April 5th to Richard Dike to make, seal, and issue Gold and Silver Thread, also for three years. The Company of Merchant Adventurers about this time petitioned for the removal of the prohibition of the import of Gold and Silver Thread.

H. C. J., vol. i. p. 511.

Two years afterwards, viz. in 1620, the attention of the House of Commons was drawn to the affairs of the Wyre-Drawers, in consequence of complaints brought against the Patent restraining the importation of Venice Gold, and for making Gold and Silver Lace and Thread, and the matter was referred to a Committee of Grievances.

Cobbett's Parliamentary History, vol. i. p. 1198.

Sir W. Spencer, stating "that Gold and Silver Thread to the value of "£60,000 in a year was made and used, a third part of which would "make good Bullion, and that the Patent against the importation of "foreign Gold and Silver Lace and Thread hindered the importation "of so much as would amount to £20,000 per annum, and £20,000 per "annum being already employed, the loss to the kingdom amounted to "£40,000 yearly." *

Sir Edward Sackville remarked, "That with regard to the parties "to whom the Patent for Gold and Silver Lace and Thread "(? were granted) His Majesty cannot do it himself but must refer "it, and moved: 'That it may be examined by the Committee, so "'that His Majesty may be cleared, and the saddle set on the right "'horse.'"

H. C. J., vol. i. p. 536.

A long discussion then took place with regard to the escape of Sir G. Mompesson, one of the Patentees, and the two others, viz. Dike and Fowle, were ordered to be committed to safe custody.

Ibid.

Sir G. Mompesson was then expelled from the House, and his partner and accomplice, Sir F. Mitchell, and Sir Henry Yelverton, the Attorney-General (who had settled the terms of the Patent) were ordered to be examined at the Tower; the confession which the latter then made has already been referred to.

Ibid.

The abuses with which the Patentees were charged, consisted in having mixed lead with the Gold and Silver Thread; and, secondly, that "Where they were to melt no Bullion here for it but to be "imported by them, they melted all here and imported none."

Ibid.

Another very long discussion ensued. The Patentees petitioned the

* The Author does not vouch for the correctness of Sir W. Spencer's deduction.

House, and were examined by it, and their misdeeds, extortions, and tyannical conduct exposed.

Commissions of Oyer and Terminer sat, and the evidence of workmen was taken, testifying to the length of time during which they had exercised the art of making Gold wire. Thos Williams stated that the Art of making Gold and Silver Thread was exercised by the Goldsmiths' Trade for fifteen years before His Majesty's accession, and that he had made Gold Wire for twenty years, and his master twenty years before him. Herrenden, a very old man, likewise stated that he had made Gold Wire for above fifty years. An Act of Common Council, dated 3rd Edward IV., referring to "Gold Drawers," was mentioned in the House by the Recorder.

Finally, the Committee resolved unanimously, "That the Patents "9° and 13° Jac. I., the two Proclamations, and the Indentures of 16° "and 18° Jac. I. were grievances both in the creation and execution." And reported that it was of opinion that a message should be sent to acquaint the Lords of Sir G. Mompesson's malpractices. Cobbett's Parliamentary History, pp. 1198-1255, and H. L. J., vol. iii. pp. 33B, and onward.

The House of Commons then asked for the assistance of the House of Lords in this matter, who appointed a Committee to confer with the Commons. The Lords also appointed a special Committee to consider the grievance of the Patents relating to Gold and Silver Thread.

Very great importance appears to have been attached by the Upper House to this question, for it devoted a considerable portion of the Session to its consideration.

An exhaustive report of these proceedings is contained in the Journals of the House of Lords, and a very interesting account of the matter is given in Vol. I. of Cobbett's "Parliamentary History," pp. 1198-1255.

In the end Sir G. Mompesson was found guilty, and sentenced " to be degraded of the Order of Knighthood, to be perpetually out-" lawed, to be imprisoned for life,—to be fined £10,000, and to be ever " held an infamous person." To which punishment the King considerately added that of "perpetual banishment," a sentence which, with wise forethought, Sir Giles had already passed upon himself. Sir Francis Mitchell, Mompesson's partner and accomplice, was sentenced " to be degraded of the Order of Knighthood, to be imprisoned during " the King's pleasure, and to be fined £1000." And Sir Henry Yelverton, who had been concerned in the granting and enforcing of these patents, was sentenced " to imprisonment in the Tower, a fine of " £4000, and a declaration of unfitness and disability to hold the place " of Attorney-General."

The King, speaking of the three Patents complained of, and of which that relating to Gold and Silver Thread was one, thus expresses himself :—

" My purpose is to strike them all dead, and (that time may not be "lost) I will have it done presently.   That of Gold and Silver " Thread was most vilely executed, both for wrongs done to men's "persons and also for abuse in the stuff, for it was a kind of false coin. " I have already freed the persons that were in prison.   I will now also "damn the Patent; and this may seem instead of pardon.   All these " three I will have recalled by Proclamation, and wish you to advise of " the fittest form for that purpose."

Rüding's
Annals of the
Coinage, p.
377.

Analytical
Index of the
Remembran-
cia.

Accordingly, on March 30, 1621, a Proclamation was made withdrawing the Patent granted to Mompesson and Mitchell.   And in June of the same year a letter was sent by the Lords of the Council to the Lord Mayor, informing him that it had been thought fit, by reason of their having been questioned in Parliament, to call in the Patents for making Gold and Silver Thread and Gold Folliat, and that His Majesty himself condemned them.   The Lord Mayor was therefore required to take steps to remove from the custody of persons in the City of London so using them, all tools and instruments used for making such Thread, etc.

Ibid.

However, the Lords of the Council soon discovered that since the calling in of the " aforesaid Patent," divers parcels of false and deceitful Gold and Silver Thread had been imported from foreign parts, especially from the Low Countries, and sold in England.   The Lord Mayor was informed of this in July, 1621, and was required to make a strict search from time to time for such parcels of Gold and Silver Thread imported, and also to take bond of the persons in whose hands they should be found, to appear before the Court of Star Chamber.

Library of the
British
Museum.

In the following year, viz. on June 11, 1622, another Proclamation was made restraining the exportation, waste, and consumption of Coin and Bullion ; " . . . and for that the making of Gold and Silver

" Thread is found to be a great waste and consumption of Coyne and
" Bullion of the Realme, therefore His Majestie doth further prohibit
" . . . all making of Gold and Silver Thread, etc., etc." " Dated,
" Greenwich 11th June, and 20th year of our Reign."

Immediately following upon this came a request for the King's _{Cal. of State}
signature to a lease to Sir Edward Villiers of the Customs on Gold and ^{Papers.}
Silver Thread imported, at a rent of £250 per annum ; also a lease of
4½d. out of the 6d. granted to the King by the " Corporation of Wyer-
drawers " on every ounce of Gold and Silver used in manufacture, and
of 4d. on the seal of every pound of thread, for the same rent ; and
coupled with this was a petition of the " Wyer-drawers' Corporation "
for the grant to their officers of 1½d. out of the 6d. tax.   Directions _{Ibid.}
appear to have been at once given to the Attorney-General to draw up
the grant as requested, to Sir E. Villiers and the " Wyer-drawers'
Company," and in the following month (September) this grant of a lease
of the customs and subsidies on Gold and Silver Thread, similar to a
grant heretofore made to Roger Pennell and Richard Grimstone, was
accorded to Sir E. Villiers on condition of his surrender of the place of
Master Worker of the Mint.

These references are interesting as showing that, even at this early
date, and in spite of the confusion arising from the granting of so many
monopolies and licenses, the " Wyer-drawers " were a sufficiently homo-
geneous body to be recognized by the official mind as a Corporation or
Company, a circumstance of which they were shrewd enough to take
advantage, for almost immediately afterwards Matthias Fowle, and
some seventy-six others, approached the King with a petition praying
that they might be made a Fellowship and body corporate and politic
in deed and in name.   The Goldsmiths about this time, viz. June, 1623,
" submitted reasons about the manufacture of Gold and Silver Thread,
" viz. : That the Refiners should not be allowed the sole right of pre-
" paring Gold for disgrossing."

This petition was favourably reported upon by the Privy Council, _{Records of the}
_{Mint, Book I.}
and by an Order. made at Whitehall in April, 1623. the Attorney- _{pp. 45-51.}
General was required to draw up a book for making a Corporation
according to the following conditions, viz. : " That an equal amount of
" Foreign Coin and Bullion should be imported from abroad to counter-

" vail that used in the saide manufactures, and that a duty of sixpence
" per ounce be paid upon all Gold and Silver Wyer used in the saide
" Manufactures, and of fourpence for the scale of every marke or pound
" of Gold and Silver Thread made up."

These instructions were duly carried out, and on June 16, 1623, a
full and complete Charter of Incorporation was granted to the Gold
and Silver Wyre-Drawers, or as they were then termed " Gould Wyer-
" Drawers of the City of London."

Patent Roll,
21 James I.
Part II. No. 8. This Charter, a summary of which is given in the Appendix, was
found by the Author when searching the Rolls at the Public Record
Office, and an attested " Office Copy " of which is now in the possession
of the Company.

Cal. of State
Papers. The above-mentioned Charter was confirmed by a Royal Proclamation of even date in the following terms :—

" G^t Britain and Ireland

" James I. King.

" By the King. A Proclamation concerning Wyer, Thread, and
" other Manufactures of Gold and Silver.

" The King being careful to prevent all unnecessary waste of Coyne
" and Bullion within the Realm, hath published sundry Proclamations
" for suppressing all irregular and unlawful melting and refining of Gold
" and Silver, and the making of Gold and Silver Thread, but not
" having succeeded, hath resolved to proceed by reducing those trades
" under order and Government, and hath granted a Charter of Incor-
" poration to the Governor, Assistants, and Commonaltie of Gold Wyer-
" Drawers of the Citie of London, etc.

" Given at our Court at Greenwich, the sixteenth day of June, in
" the one and twentieth yeare of our Reigne of Great Britaine, France
" and Ireland. God save the King ! "

See Edmond-
son's Heraldry
and Berry's
Encyclopædia
Heraldica. Having obtained their Charter, and succeeded in getting themselves
numbered with the incorporated Guilds of the City of London, it
might fairly have been thought that the storm-tossed and harassed
Wyer-Drawers had at last got into port ; and that, having found a
haven of peace and security, they might have been at liberty to pursue
their trade without further let or hindrance ; but alas for the futility of
human expectations ! scarcely had the seal upon their Charter found

time to set, when fresh troubles arose, for in less than nine months after the date of the granting of this Charter, a Bill "for ratifying and con- H. C. Journals, vol. i. p. 726. "firming His Majesty's Charter to the Company of Gold Wyer- " Drawers of the City of London" having been brought into the House of Commons, the House, which it would seem was then in a most intractable mood, and evidently still cherished a lively recollection of the embittered discussions and proceedings which had taken place some four years previously, unceremoniously rejected this Bill, and ordered the Patent of the Gold Wyer-Drawers to be brought in to the Committee of Grievances.

This Committee reported that "The Patent of Gold Wyer- Ibid., p. 753. "Drawers was void in itself, and made upon three false suggestions," and it resolved "That it was a grievance in creation and execu- "tion." Sir Edward Villiers explained "He did farm the customs of "Gold and Silver Thread to the King for a valuable consideration." The House thereupon resolved "That the Patent of the new Incor- "poration of Wyer-Drawers was a grievance," and ordered "that "precedents should be looked up to see what punishments had in like "cases been inflicted." It also ordered "that Matthias Fowle (the "first Governor of the New Company) be committed to the custody of "the Serjeant."

The House of Commons then petitioned the King in the following Cobbett's Parliamentary History, vol. i. p. 1490. terms :—

"The Petition of the Commons on Grievances.

"22 Jac I. 1624.

"Gold Wyer Drawers—Whereas within the City of London there "was an ancient art and trade of Gold Wyer Drawing exercised by "divers being members of the corporation of Goldsmiths of London, "whereby they maintained not only themselves and their families, but "also set many other persons on work, until one, Matthias Fowle, and "others (men never bound apprentices in the said trade according to "law) obtained from your Majesty letters patent bearing date 14th "June in the 21st year of your reign, whereby they were incorporated "by the names of Gold Wyer Drawers of the City of London, the "Governor, the Assistants, and the Commonaltie; upon suggestion "that they would import from foreign parts, to be converted into

" current coin of this Kingdom, so much foreign Gold and Silver Coin
" and Bullion as should countervail the Bullion they should use in
" making the Gold Wyer and other manufactures; and also that the
" same Gold Wyer should be of a sufficient goodness and sold at the
" like or cheaper rate than the same was before the said new Corpora-
" tion ; and by the said letters patent the said Gold Wyer Drawers
" anciently brought up to and using the said trade were prohibited to
" use and exercise the same any more.   And further your Majesty by
" the said letters patent, at the prayer of the persons so newly incor-
" porated, did impose 6^d upon every ounce of Gold Wyer that should
" be made or sold by them within this Realm.

    " The humble petition of your subjects is—' That your Majesty will
" ' be graciously pleased to publish and declare the same accordingly ;
" ' and that the said letters patent should never hereafter be put in
execution.' "

    The King, on receipt of this petition, appears to have once more
veered round, and accordingly on July 10, 1624, he issued another
Proclamation to the following effect :—

Proclamation
in Library of
the British
Museum,
506, II. 11
25.   " His Majesty, in consequence of complaints of the Commons, and
" report by the Lords of the Privy Council, declares the Wyer-drawers
" Charter to be null and void, and announces his intention to abolish
" the Manufacture of Gold and Silver Thread, etc., as being wasteful of
" the Coin and Bullion of the Realm."

H. L. Jour-
nals, vol. iii.
p. 415b,
22 Jac. I.
1624.   In consequence of this the Wyer-drawers petitioned the House of
Lords for the return of the Bonds which they had given in accordance
with the terms of their Charter ; which was granted.

Cal. of State
Papers.   Sir E. Villiers at the same time obtained an annuity of £1000 on
condition that he surrendered his grant of the sums to be paid to the
Crown by the Company of Gold Wyer-Drawers of London.

Ibid.   Notwithstanding the King's Proclamation of the 10th July, this
manufacture appears to have continued, for in the same year, Lady
Roxburgh petitioned for a license to assay all Gold and Silver Thread
in the " Bar" before it was manufactured, and pointed out how this
license differed from that of the Earl of Holland, which was to assay
the Thread after it was made.

    Upon the death of the King and the accession of Charles I. there

ensued a lull in the agitation which for such a lengthened period had
disturbed the Gold and Silver Wyer-drawing trade, the only mention of
the industry during the next ten years being a petition by Sir Nicholas
Salter for relief from his debts, amounting to many thousands of pounds,
arising from his having been engaged as surety for the Agents of Gold
and Silver Thread; and a petition by Lady Barbara Villiers, widow,
praying for a discharge of the arrears of rent due upon a lease dated June
29, 1627, for twenty-one years, of the duties on the importation of Gold
and Silver Thread. It was conceived that these duties must decay, for
the reason that it (? Thread and Lace) was better made here than could
be imported, and it was ascertained that the duty received by Lady
Villiers in eighteen months only amounted to £257, whereas Sir Wm.
Garway (? Garraway), used to collect £1246 annually. There were also
two Royal Proclamations, dealing with the industry, issued during this
period. One on the 4th of February, 3 Car I. "To prevent abuses
"and waste in making Gold and Silver Thread;" and the other on
May 3rd of the same year, "Prohibiting the melting of the coin for
"the purpose of making Thread."

About the commencement of the year 1635, the old agitation
in the trade broke out with increased intensity; it began with a
complaint made by the Goldsmiths on January 25, 163⅘, to the
King and Privy Council, pointing out the detriment and damage caused
by the undue practices of certain Gold Wyer-Drawers and Refiners in
melting the Coin and Bullion of the Realm. This was followed by a
petition of the Wyer-Drawers in March of this year, and again on the
16th of April, "asking for a Corporation," and offering as an inducement
to pay the King £1000 per annum, and 2d. per ounce for every ounce
of such bullion and foreign specie (? melted and used).

The King at once appointed a Commission of Inquiry into the
abuses complained of, viz. on April 17th, 1635, and referred the
petition of the Wyer-Drawers to Sir John Banks, Attorney-General,
who reported favourably to the proposal, and after many treaties with
the Wyer-Drawers, "modelled a certificate recommending their incor-
"poration under certain conditions." This immediately led to a petition
from the Wardens and Commonalty of the Goldsmiths, who on the
12th of June, "Prayed a reference to the Council, that in incorporat-

Margin notes:
Cal. of State Papers, 1625-6.

Ibid., 1629.

Ibid.

Thomas Violet's "Appeal to Cæsar," published 1660.

Thomas Violet's Tracts, published 1656.

Ibid., published 1653 and 1656.

Cal. of State Papers (Domestic Series). Thomas Violet's Tracts.

Cal. of State Papers.

"ing the Wyer-Drawers, the rights of the Petitioners might be pre-
"served."

Opposition also started up in another quarter, for, to quote the words
of one "Thomas Violet," Goldsmith, of London, whose history for the
ensuing five or six years is inextricably mixed up with that of the
Wyer-Drawers, and who, shortly after his release from the Tower, viz.
in 1653 and 1656, wrote several pamphlets addressed to The Lord
Protector, relating his experiences in connection with the Gold and
Silver Wyer-Drawers, and making sundry proposals for the regulation
and reformation of the Trade ; which pamphlets are preserved in the
Libraries of the British Museum, and of the Corporation of the City
of London, and contain much very interesting information about the
doings of the Wyer-Drawers during this period :

Continuing the story then in the words of Thomas Violet, "The
"Refiners, viz. Alderman Sir John Wollaston, Master Alderman Gibbs,
"and others, seeing the Wyer-Drawers go about to exclude them of
"their trade, did serve the Wyer-Drawers as the Merchant Adventurers
"did the Clothworkers, viz. outbid them.   For they agreed, amongst
"other things, to pay sixpence per ounce duty on all Gold and Silver-
"Gilt Wyer.   Thus the Wyer-Drawers, who would have excluded the
"Refiners from their Corporation, would by these Articles be debarred
"their Trade, and both Goldsmiths and Wyer-drawers be prevented
"from preparing any Silver for the manufactures of the Wyer-
"Drawers."

Thomas
Violet's
Tracts.
In the meantime the Commission of Inquiry appointed by the King
in April, 1635, having commenced its labours, a great number of abuses
were speedily discovered, and many persons found themselves in
trouble ; amongst them, Aldermen Wollaston and Gibbs, and also
Violet himself, who suffered twenty weeks' imprisonment for refusing to
answer interrogatories ; to the loss of his trade, which he speaks of as
being then "Greater than any Goldsmith's in London."

Ibid.
Chastened by this punishment, Violet appears to have made his
peace with the Privy Council ; and the King, having heard of Violet's
successful and profitable method of dealing with the exportation of
Gold and Silver Bullion and Coin, complimented him upon his
ingenuity, and His Majesty expressed his willingness "to share stakes

"with him," by relieving him of £2000, that being the price of his pardon.

The King was so pleased with Violet's skill in managing Mint Thomas business and the Bullion of the Nation, that he also appointed him Violet's Surveyor of the Manufacture of Gold and Silver Wyer and Thread, on condition of receiving a royalty of £4000 per annum. This grant, which was made in 163$\frac{3}{6}$, cost Violet nearly £1500.

Shortly previous to this, viz. on September 30, 1635, a Procla- Library of the British mation was issued, "ordering the Sealing of Gold and Silver Thread, Museum. "Purles, Cut worke, and Bone-laces, and appointing Mr. Thos Smith "deputy for the Sealing."

Consequent upon this, viz. December 9, 1635, came a petition from Cal. of State Papers the Governor and Company of the Silkmen, who were incorporated in (Domestic 1631; one of the conditions (? of incorporation) being "that they Series). "persume not to challenge any interest in determining the fineness or "coarseness of the bullion which is wrought into Gold and Silver "Thread, knowing that the Government thereof had long since been "conferred upon the Incorporation of Goldsmiths—Nevertheless the "Petitioners conceive themselves concerned in giving rules for the well "making of Gold and Silver Thread, and such silks as belong thereto, "and pray relief from the recent Proclamation preventing them from "doing so."

About this time the King, in a letter to the Attorney-General, Ibid. recites an indenture dated June 29, 1627, granting to Lady Barbara Villiers, widow, for twenty-one years, all customs payable on Gold and Silver Thread; and ordering that a Commission be appointed to prosecute all offenders against this grant.

Another Commission was, on January 3, 163$\frac{3}{6}$, issued to the Lords Cal. of State Papers. of the Treasury to see to the execution of the Proclamations for the regulation of the business of Gold and Silver Thread; and on the 18th of January a fresh Proclamation was made, "Against the deceitful Cal. of State Papers, and "making of Gold and Silver Thread. No English coin or bullion was Syllabus in English of "to be used therein, and all Gold and Silver Thread was ordered to be Rymer's "made up in skeins, and all such manufactures were to be brought to Foedera. "Commissioners to be sealed." On the following day, Thomas Cal. of State Papers. Violet's petition to be granted the office of Sealing and Surveying all

Gold and Silver and Copper Wyer and Thread was referred to the Attorney-General to prepare a bill granting this office to — Johnson, — Rich, and Violet.

Reverting now to the petition of the Refiners, viz. Aldermen Wollaston and Gibbs, and others, who were seeking to forestall the Wyer-Drawers, but who themselves were in trouble in consequence of the proceedings of the Commission of Inquiry, the matter is seen to be under the consideration of the Committee for Trade (*vide* Mr. Secretary Windebank's notes of the proceedings) ; and the two Aldermen, to again quote Thomas Violet, " Feeling themselves exposed to the Law, " petitioned the King for his Grace and Mercy."

Violet (by his own account) did his best to obtain this pardon, and his efforts—how requited the story will show—coupled with a lavish expenditure of money, seem to have been successful, for shortly afterwards, viz. on May 16, 1636, the indenture between the King on the one part, and the two Aldermen and six others, on the other part, was duly sealed ; and the King, in consideration of the large sum of money that had been paid, and of the further amounts that would be paid to him in the shape of duty, was, according to Violet, " pleased to gratify " them with a courtly title, calling them ' His well beloved subjects ' " ' The Refiners of London, His Agents.' " This arrangement conferred upon these eight persons the sole right of preparing all the Gold and Silver to be used by the Spinners and Lace-men of London ; and Violet estimated the annual value of this Gold and Silver that they were thus authorized to prepare, at £100,000.

So great a monopoly at once aroused a most determined opposition. The Wardens and Company of Goldsmiths repeatedly complained of it to the King and Privy Council in 1636, 37, 38, and 39, as being contrary to the Statute of 21 Jac. I. cap. iii. ; and several influential Goldsmiths also came forward to oppose this interference with their trade, and submitted proposals for its removal. The Refiners, however, appear to have claimed and maintained their rights as Agents for the King.

In January of this year (1636), a Commission was also issued to William, Archbishop of Canterbury ; the Earl of Manchester, Keeper of the Privy Seal ; Lord Goring, Master of the Horse; and twenty

Margin notes:
Thomas Violet's Tracts.

Cal. of State Papers.

Thomas Violet's Tracts.

Ibid.

Ibid.

Syllabus in English of Rymer's Fœdera.

others, to enforce the observance of the Proclamation concerning the manufacture of Gold and Silver Thread ; and on the 4th of July of the Syllabus in English of Rymer's Fœdera. same year, a Commission was given to Sir Egremont Thynne, and thirteen others, to try frauds and deceits in the payment of customs on Gold and Silver Thread.

In July of 1637, a book of entries relating to the accounts of Sir Cal. of State Papers (Domestic Series). Robert Rich, — Johnson, and Thos. Violet, Receivers of Profits and Duties payable to His Majesty by the Wyer-Drawers, was produced to the Council ; and a note sets out that these profits were charged with the payment of £300 per annum to the Countess of Roxburgh, and £500 per annum to the Earl of Holland.*

On the 10th of September of the same year the Commissioners for Cal. of State Papers. regulating the manufacture of Gold and Silver Thread, reported that there were many offenders against the Proclamations and Orders ; and the Attorney-General was instructed to prosecute. And on the same day the Refiners, appointed for providing the Gold and Silver used in Ibid. making Thread, submitted a proposal concerning a more convenient way of issuing the same by freedom being allowed to every one of them to sell at a place appointed. This proposal was duly acceded to ; and the alteration was made in the indenture between His Majesty and the Refiners.

In January of the following year, viz. 163⅞, W. Clerk, a Gold Ibid. Wyer-Drawer, petitioned the King, stating that " He had brought the " Copper Wire manufacture to perfection ; thus saving His Majesty's " Bullion, nevertheless his premises had been broken open, his goods " seized, and his servants imprisoned." He prayed for pardon and the restitution of his occupation, which was granted.

In 1639 a note in the hand of Mr. Secretary Windebank sets out Ibid. " That the manufacture of Gold and Silver Thread will consume great " quantities of Bullion. If the Trade be left at large, every one " will be desirous to import Bullion to furnish this market, so that the " manufacture will be supplied and the Mint continually furnished with " Bullion enough."

The contest between the Goldsmiths, Gold Wyer-Drawers, Violet's Tracts, published 1653 and 1656. Refiners, and Spinners is referred to by Violet as having lasted from

* Both of these grants have been previously referred to.

1635 to 1640; and whilst it was going on, the King and Lords of the Privy Council "cast about how to be truly informed of all these "abuses, and to search into the bottom of all this knavery and "cheating." They therefore empowered Violet, under the Great Seal, to make search for and seize all bad Gold and Silver Thread and Wyer; to deface it, and inform against the offenders. Assays were ordered to be taken by Mr. Jackson, Assay Master at Goldsmiths Hall, under Violet's directions; the King's standard at this time being 11 oz. 2 dwt. of Fine Silver to the pound.

Violet, according to his own account, appears to have discharged the duties of his office as Surveyor with the greatest zeal, fearlessness, and impartiality; and it was testified that, during the period when he exercised this supervision, Gold and Silver Thread and Wyer was better made than it had been either before or since.

This energetic officer narrates how he prosecuted the Queen's Silkman, and but for the direct intervention of Her Majesty, would have made an example of him; he even seized 50 lbs. of Silver Lace, mixed with copper, which was found in the possession of Alderman Garraway whilst he was Lord Mayor of London. Aldermen Wollaston and Gibbs and the other monopolist Refiners also received a share of his attention, and he mentions that he placed several offenders in the pillory.

The meeting of the Long Parliament in November, 1640, provided the opportunity for once more drawing attention to the insufferable grievances caused by the monopolists. The Wyer-Drawers again complained and clamoured against the regulation, and petitioned Parliament against the Monopoly, their petition being referred by the Committee of Grievances to the Committee for Trade.

Upon the matter being considered by the House of Commons, the King took the part of the Refiners, whom he called " His sheep," and designated the Wyer-Drawers as " His Goats ;" but notwithstanding this powerful opposition, the Wyer-Drawers boldly told His Majesty that " They would submit to the Law but not to the ' Refiners ' " Monopoly."

Violet also charged Alderman Wollaston with having defrauded the King of nearly £3000 yearly, from 1630 to 1640, he being then

II. C. J., vol. ii. p. 43 (16 Car i. Dec. 2, 1640), also pp. 20 and 310, giving references to Commissioners appointed for the regulating of the Trade.

Thomas Violet's Tracts.

"Melter of the Mint, and as such, the servant of the Master-Worker Thomas
"of the Mint; nevertheless he made more than all the principal Violet's Tracts.
"officers of the Mint twice told ; and although a servant, it was
"the profits of his place that principally raised him to be an
"Alderman."

The King, on being informed of this, became very angry, and
swore at his officers of the Mint, calling them "either knaves or fools ;"
he then appointed Violet to be Master of the Mint at a Fee of £500
a year ; and also put him in Alderman Wollaston's place there.

The Refiners, viz. "Agents," finding that many of the Members Ibid.
of the House of Commons resented the restriction of the Trade
to a few Refiners, "cunningly" put in a petition to Parliament on
November 24, 1640, "complaining that the prices allowed to them to
"sell their Silver, and their position as Agents, had been forcibly put
"upon them." A statement which Violet at once shows to have
been untrue, by pointing out "that they might easily have forfeited
"their Agency in eight, or any eight days, by omitting to conform to
"the conditions of their contract ; instead of which, they kept it up
"for their own profit, thus depriving the Goldsmiths and the Wyer-
"Drawers of a free market."

As a result of the Parliamentary proceedings, and subsequent Cal. of State Papers.
lengthy examination by the Attorney-General and the rest of the
King's Council at Law, and before the Lords of the Council, it was,
"after many great and grave disputes, unanimously carried, that the
"intrusting of the Regulation of this Manufacture of Gold and Silver
"Wyer and Thread was not to be done by way of Corporation, neither
"to the Refiners nor Wyer-Drawers." The reasons assigned being,
"That the assays made by the Assay Master of Goldsmiths Hall
"showed that the manufacture was coarse and adulterated and below
"the Standard,—and also that the English Thread was slightly made
"and not so substantial and serviceable as that imported from Venice
"and other foreign parts."

The Lords of the Council then made a rule that "no Gold and
"Silver Thread should be under 5 oz. Silver to 3 oz. Silk ; and for
"needle thread 6 oz. Silver to 3 oz. Silk." Another rule was also made,
"That the Thread should be done up in skeins of one ounce weight,

"and sealed as was the Venice custom; which had made those
"manufactures so celebrated that they passed all the world over."
The King and his Council "also granted to Tho' Violet a seal, which
"was 'the Rose and Crown,' to seal all Thread in skeins, as a
"warranty to the nation; the other end of the skein bearing the
"workman's seal."

That Violet's office was no sinecure is proved by the fact that he
estimated the amount of Gold and Silver Thread that passed under his
seal during the four or five years when he was Surveyor, at above one
million skeins; and in another passage he calculated that "at that
"time the yearly value of the stuff out of the Silkmen's shops in
"London, when it was made into Lace, Ribbons, Spangles, etc., was
"above £200,000 as it passed his seal and survey."

The troublous times that shortly afterwards ensued; the flight of
the King from London; the espousal of the cause of Parliament by
the citizens and merchants of this City, and the outbreak of the Civil
War, soon diverted men's attention to more serious matters than that
of personal adornment, and consequently the Wyer-Drawers appear to
have been left very much to themselves, and with but little demand
for their manufactures.

Just about this time, however, Alderman Wollaston, who had early
taken side with Parliament, and who was then, 164¾, Lord Mayor of
London, saw his chance to be revenged upon Violet. The latter
having, as he states, been decoyed into bringing a letter from the King
at Oxford to the Lord Mayor of London, he was denounced to Parliament as a malignant. The Lord Mayor and Alderman Gibbs, whose
pardons Violet had been instrumental in obtaining from the King some
six or seven years previously, being the chief informers against him at
a Common Hall held at Guildhall; and, to quote Violet's own words,
"He was on their unjust information committed to the Tower as a
"malignant on the 6th January 164¾, where he remained in close con-
"finement for nearly four years. He was sequestrated of his estate,
"and damnified and plundered to the value of £8000." His great
enemy, on the other hand, having joined the Roundheads, soon became
a power in the State, and was shortly afterwards appointed chief of
the War Department of the Treasury.

Cal. of State
Papers
(Domestic
Series).

The only other mention of the Wyer-Drawers, down to the commencement of the Commonwealth, is by Violet, who states that "An "Ordinance of Parliament was made on the 6th August 1641 (when "he was in the Tower) for all Gold and Silver Wyer to pay 4*d.* per "ounce Troy at the disgrossing at the Bar; and that all Gold and "Silver to be disgrossed, be brought to a certain place appointed."

Violet's Tracts, published 1653.

This ordinance seemed to have deterred many of the Refiners from practising their Trade; others, less scrupulous, disregarded it; and Violet calculated that in four years there remained in the hands of the Wyer-Drawers and Refiners some £20,000 arrears of Excise due to the State.

CHAPTER V.

HE principal information as to the doings of the Wyer-Drawers during this period is to be found in Violet's pamphlets, published in 1653 and 1656 (and already frequently referred to), when, some years after his release from the Tower, he was applying to Parliament, and especially to the Council for Trade, for the restoration of his estate and his re-appointment to the offices of Surveyor of the Manufacture of Gold and Silver Wyer and Thread, and of Master-worker and Melter at the Mint; and offering to accept these offices at the original scale of Fees as part payment of the sums promised to him for services rendered to the State in connection with the seizure of three vessels in the Thames which were laden with Specie and Bullion about to be exported from the country.

Cal. of State Papers.

Much attention appears to have been given by Parliament to this matter, for, in a subsequent pamphlet published by Violet in 1660, viz. "His Appeal to Cæsar," he cites the report of the Committee (of Parliament) made in 1657, wherein the great abuses practised in melting down current silver coins of the Nation for making Lace, and the frauds committed upon the weavers of the same, were complained of; and, as a remedy against these evils, the reappointment of Violet to his old office was recommended.

The Lord Protector referred the question to the Privy Council in 1658; but his death occurring shortly afterwards, Violet renewed his application to Richard Cromwell, who in his turn referred the matter for consideration and report; which was, "That Thomas Violet "deserved well of his country; he should be paid his claims; and that "he was a fit and useful person to be employed either at the Mint or "in the office for the regulating of Gold and Silver Wyre, Thread, and "Lace."

Reverting now to the commencement of the period of the Common-wealth, the question of Gold Wyer-Drawing appears to have been re-opened by the following petition, a copy of which is preserved in the "Choice Library of the Corporation of the City of London :— Scraps," vol. i. p. 92.

"The Humble petition of the Refiners and Gold Wyer-Drawers of "London.

"To the Supreme Authority of this Nation, the Parliament of the "Commonwealth of England.

"Your Petitioners therefore most humbly pray that they may have "by Authority of Parliament a Charter granted unto them, and may "thereby be incorporated into a body politic, consisting of one Master, "three Wardens, twelve Assistants, and Commonalty; and thereby "have power to bring all the parties of the said Trade and Arts into "order; with such other grants and privileges as may be for the well "regulating of the said Manufactures, Trade and Arts, and the "members of their Corporation.

"And your Petitioners shall pray, etc.

"Dated. 1650."

This matter was evidently referred to Violet for report; for in his pamphlets he speaks of the draft of a Corporation presented at this time to the Council for Trade, as being, as desired by them, viz. the Refiners, and Gold Wyer-Drawers, "utterly destructive to the "Commonwealth."

Then follow a series of references to the proceedings of 1635–40, Violet's and a number of suggestions as to how the Thread should be spun; Tracts. the quantity of wheels to be used; the relative proportion of Silver to

Silk ; and the strict division of the Trades ; viz. " No Wyer-Drawer to
" make Lace or Ribbon ; " and " No Weaver to make Gold and Silver
" Thread."

The grievances of the Women Spinners were also dealt with;
Violet specially denouncing "certain unlawful engines called wheels,
" which twist the silver so slightly as merely to deceive the wearers,"
and stating that "the Women Spinners, some thousands in number,
" frequently complained of them, and had moreover presented proposals
" to the Council for Trade for regulating their Art."

Violet's
Tracts.In conclusion, the opinion was expressed that " This manufacture
" will never be justly made if there be not a government settled by a
" Corporation."   That, " The number of workers in the trade be re-
" stricted."   And that " The Company be enjoined to bring in the
" value in Bullion from beyond the Seas as they waste in this manu-
" facture."

(Violet, in 1660, estimated this waste at £30,000 per annum.)

Cal. of State
Papers
(Domestic),
May, 1650.These propositions of Violet's were printed at length, and have
been preserved in the State Records ; they were also, on the 23rd of
December of the same year, viz. 1650, ordered to be referred to the
Committee of the Mint.

The following order was likewise issued :—

Violet's
Tracts, pub-
lished
1653.Die Veneris, December 20, 1650.   At the Council for Trade at
Whitehall.   Ordered, " That a model or way for the regulating the
" trade of Gold and Silver Wyer and Thread etc. be tendered to this
" Council against Friday, January 17, by the Wyer-Drawers and
" Refiners, and some of the Women-Spinners ; who are hereby required
" to meet together and consult about it.   And to take into considera-
" tion the papers presented by Master Thomas Violet."

Cal. of State
Papers.About this time, viz. December 17, 1650, Violet's petition was
referred to the Council of Trade.

Ibid.In the following year the Committee for Trade, appointed to inquire
into the abuses in the manufacture of Gold and Silver Thread and
Lace, and other Trades, made its report ; and suggested, " That a way
" be found for viewing, confirming, or rectifying the By-laws and
" Ordinances now in use by the societies of Merchants."

Ibid.About twelve months later, viz. in May, 1652, Sir Robert Stone, reporting on Mint affairs, asserted that there was great waste of Silver in England by wearing Gold and Silver Lace; and stated that £300,000 worth was made annually.

On September 13, 1655, the Commissioners for Appeals and Regulating the Excise, made a reference to "The farm of Excise" on Gold, Silver, and Copper Wire being let to Richard Babbington for £2800; and very shortly afterwards, the workers in Copper-gilt and Silver Thread petitioned the Lord Protector against the recent increase on Copper from twopence to twelvepence per pound. This petition was, in the ensuing year, followed by one from the Refiners, Gold Wyer-Drawers, and others, which was referred to a Committee, for Report, by the Excise Commissioners. Cal. of State Papers.

At the close of 1657 the Council advised the confirmation of a contract made by a Committee of Parliament, for the improvement of Customs and Excise, with Martin Noel, and Henry Quinton of London, for a lease of the duties on certain goods, amongst which were included Gold, Silver, and Copper Wyer, in England and Wales, for five years, at the sum of £65,000 a year. Ibid.

With the exception of the proceedings already referred to, relating to Violet's applications to be reinstated in his former offices, the Records make no further mention of the Wyer-Drawers or their trade, down to the close of the time of the Commonwealth.

CHAPTER VI.

T might have been expected that with the Restoration
in 1660, and the re-establishment of a Court, there
would have been a revival of the previous habits
of luxury in apparel, and a consequent increased
demand for adornments of Gold and Silver Lace,
nevertheless, the ever-present and important question of the scarcity of Coin and Bullion led to the
earliest measures taken by Charles II., with reference to this trade,
being of a nature to largely restrict its operations.

The first step appears to have been the issuing on June 10, 1661,
of a Royal Proclamation wherein the King announced his intention, in
due time, of reducing the making of Gold and Silver Thread, Lace,
etc., to good order and governance, and of diminishing the consumption
of Bullion in these manufactures.

About the same time two Bills were brought into the House of
Commons—one to prevent frauds in making Gold and Silver Lace;
the other, against the wearing of the same. The former Bill was committed, but the second reading refused; the latter was only ordered.
The mere mention of this, however, gave rise to serious apprehension,

Library of
British
Museum,
21. h i.
151
and Cal. of
State Papers.

H. C. Jour-
nals, vol. viii.
pp. 357 and
368.

and at once led to a petition from the Hand Spinners of Gold and Cal. of State Papers.
Silver Wyer, Thread, Lace, etc. to the King and Parliament, stating
that " They were in terror at the report that Parliament intended to
"put a stop to the wearing of their manufactures ;" and " Imploring
"that their trade and work might be reformed but not destroyed ;"
and begging " that the coming of the Queen from Portugal might not
" be signalized by an Act passed to ruin thousands of them."

Shortly previous to this, Thos. Violet, who, as before stated, had Ibid.
again renewed his application "to be made Registrar and Searcher of
"all Gold and Silver exported, with allowances and forfeitures, at the
" Mint," was, on the favourable report of the Officers of the Mint,
appointed to this post, and an official seal was entrusted to him. With
this appointment ended Violet's further connection with the Gold and
Silver Wyer-Drawers, whose history for the past twenty-five years had
been so intimately bound up with his own.

In the following year the Wyer-Drawers seemed likely to be taken
under still more distinguished patronage than had yet been their lot to Ibid.
experience ; for, in 166⅔, " the Maids of Honour," and the " Mother to
the King," petitioned His Majesty "to grant to Trustees named by
"them, and for their benefit, a Patent similar to the one conferred in
" the late reign, on account of the corruption of Gold and Silver Lace."

This petition was referred to the Attorney-General for report, but Ibid.
was evidently not granted ; for, a little later in the same year, John
Garrill, Wyer-Drawer, petitioned the King for a Patent for his invention of casting and preparing Gold and Silver Ingots for making Wyer
and Lace.

The matter was referred to the Lord Treasurer, and by him to the
Attorney-General, who reported in its favour, whereupon the Lord
Treasurer made a final and favourable report.

Further evidence as to this invention was taken by Sir Philip Ibid.
Warwick, " who was informed by persons able to judge, that Mr.
" Garrill's new mode of making Gold and Silver Wyer was both
" beautiful and durable, and would save one ounce in twelve ; and that
" a Patent should be granted if the invention were new."

Accordingly, on December 3, 1663, a Warrant was issued to grant Ibid.
to John Garrill the sole right of preparing Gold and Silver Ingots to be

E

drawn into Wyer for Gold and Silver Lace; and on the 29th of December the Patent was confirmed, with liberty to import foreign Gold and Silver for the purpose of his trade, and on the condition that he had his goods assayed at the Mint.

On the 27th of February of the following year, an indignation meeting of Wyer-Drawers was held at the house of Simon Urlin, Wyer-Drawer, in Gutter Lane, to denounce the above Patent; when Mr. Urlin "said, in a passion, that the granting of patents was the "cause of the late King's head being cut off." This rash remark was at once reported to the Privy Council. The State Papers, however, do not show that the speaker suffered for his temerity.

About this time the Gold and Silver Wyer-Drawers once more began to take concerted action with a view to bring about the remedying of their grievances, and the reorganization of their trade upon a sounder and better basis. This improvement they considered would be best effected "by their being Incorporated under a Royal Charter, "from His Majesty the King."

Accordingly, the following Petition was shortly afterwards drawn up and presented. Some little uncertainty exists with regard to the exact date of this Petition; the Goldsmiths' records put it as shown below, but the subsequent references prove that it must have been anterior to this.

"Friday the 6th day of June 1664.

"To the King's Most Excellent Majesty.

"The humble Petition of the Wyer-Drawers of the City of London, "and other Traders in the Manufactory of Gold and Silver Lace etc.

"Sheweth

"'That your petitioners' Art or Mystery hath been of long con-
"'tinuance, and very beneficial to the Kingdom, as also a support of
"'many thousands as have been solely maintained thereby, but is of
"'late much decayed and declined by divers persons making that
"'Manufactory slight and adulterate, which if not timely prevented,
"'will prove very prejudicial and dishonourable to the Kingdom, and
"'the absolute ruin of a multitude of persons that have gained an
"'honest livelihood thereby, the said mischief being occasioned through
"'the want of due regulation and government in the said Manufacture.

" 'Wherefore your Petitioners do humbly beseech your Sacred
" ' Majesty to take their deplorable tale into your gracious considera-
" ' tion, and to refer it to such persons as your Majesty shall think
" ' meet, that they may resolve upon such expedients for regulation of
" ' the said Manufacture as they in their wisdom shall judge most
" ' advantageous to your Kingdom, the affair being of such importance
" ' as the preservation of your Majesty's Bullion, the making the Manu-
" ' facture more beneficial and durable, and the maintenance of so many
" ' thousands of your Majesty's subjects. We in all humility beseech
" ' your Majesty's Grace and favour therein.'
" And your Petitioners shall ever pray etc."
(Then follow the signatures.)
This matter appears, from the Records of the Royal Mint, to have
been referred to "a Committee of Parliament;'" and the King subsequently made the following Order :— <small>Mint Records, book ii.</small>

" Whitehall May 4th, 1664. <small>From the Records of the Goldsmiths Company.</small>
" His Majesty is graciously pleased to refer this Petition to the
" Council of the Mint to consider the contents of the same and to make
" Report to His Majesty what they think fit to be done upon the
" humble desire of the Petitioners concerning a regulation of their
" Manufacture, and then His Majesty will declare his further pleasure.
" WILL MORICE."

The narrative is now taken up by the Records of the Royal Mint,
from which the following extracts have been made.
" May 25, 1664. Petition of Gold Wyer Drawers concerning the <small>Minute Book, No. ii.</small>
" regulation of the Manufactory of Gold and Silver Thread, Lace, etc.,
" referred by His Majesty to the Council of the Mint, then consisting of—

The Lord Treasurer	Sir Charles Harbord	Sir Ralph Freeman
Lord Ashley	Sir Heneage Finch	Henry Slingsby Esq,
Lord Brouncker	Sir Henry Vernon	Wm Aerskin Esq,
Sir Paul Neale	Sir Robet Moray	Thomas Henshaw Esq
Sir Wm Compton	Sir Wm Parkhurst,	Robert Boyle Esq
James Hoare Esq, and Dr Jonathan Goddard.		

Ordered. " That the Wardens and Assistants of the Goldsmiths

" Company, the Barrmen who doe usually disgrosse the Silver and Glit
" Wyer, Some of the Spinners, and the Petitioners, doe attend before
" them on the first day of June then ensuing, in order that the Council
" might take into consideration the establishing and regulating of the
" saide Manufacture of Gold and Silver Thread."

June 1, 1664. At the request of the Wardens and Assistants of
the Goldsmiths Company, a copy of the Arguments and Reasons of the
Wyer-Drawers was given to them, and the 15th day of June was
appointed for the consideration of proposals for regulating the saide
Manufactures. The Council also decided to make trials and assays of
the samples of Wyer submitted by the Petitioning Wyer-Drawers, and
were assisted therein by John Garrill, Wyer-Drawer.

June 15, 1664. The Wardens and Assistants of the Goldsmiths
Company delivered their answers to the proposals of the Wyer-Drawers,
but asked for further time to consider the desire of the Council of the
Mint " about receiving the saide Wyer-Drawers into their Company,
and making them one body incorporate with them."

Accordingly Wednesday, the 29th of June, was fixed for receiving
these answers ; all papers were to be produced, and likewise the proceedings of the late Committee of Parliament dealing with this matter.
And the saide Wyer-Drawers, Refiners, Barrmen, Spinners, Weavers,
and others, were ordered to attend.

June 29, 1664. The Goldsmiths Company desired a further day
for the delivery of their answer, their Council having been unable to
consider the matter ; and were given until Wednesday, July 13.

July 13, 1664. No report of this meeting is recorded, but a short
entry, dated September 5th, states that the Wyer-Drawers were
ordered to attend the Council on September 9th. The Mint Records
of this period, however, end at September 5th.

The story of this interesting episode in the history of the Wyer-
Drawers is now continued in the Records of the Worshipful Company
of Goldsmiths ; extracts from which have, with very great courtesy,
been furnished to the author. The first is as follows :—

" Wednesday the xxjth of September 1664.

" At this Court the Committee which was appointed at the last
" Court of Assistants to consider and report in answer in writing to the

"paper of the particular powers desired by the Refiners and Wire-
" Drawers in order to an Incorporation, presented the same to the con-
" sideration of this Court, the tenor whereof is as followeth.

   " The particulars of the powers which the Refiners and Gold-wire-
" drawers of London desire to have by an Incorporation."

   The Minute then recites the heads of a complete draft Charter of
Incorporation, consisting of nineteen clauses, which had been drawn
up by the Wyer-Drawers, and with which powers they humbly prayed
that His Majesty would be pleased to incorporate them.

   These powers were very similar to those contained in the Charter
of 1693, and under which the Gold and Silver Wyre-Drawers Company
have acted down to the present day ; and there can be little doubt that
this draft Charter served as a model for the one that was at last
definitely granted some nineteen years later. The entry then sets out
in the following terms :—

   " The answers of the Wardens and Assistants of the Company of
" Goldsmiths, London, to the paper presented by the Refiners and
" Wire-drawers to the Right Honourable the Lords and others of the
" Council of His Majesty's Mint, touching sundry powers which they
" desire to have by an Incorporation."

   To which they humbly offer by way of objection these reasons
following :—

   1st. They say that the search, oversight, assay and government of
all manner of Gold and Silver wrought and to be wrought and put to
sale throughout England, is a power and privilege anciently granted to
the Wardens of the Company of Goldsmiths by Charters and Acts of
Parliament, and therefore not to be communicated to the Refiners and
Wire-drawers.

   2nd. The abuses of the Wire-drawers in their trades the Goldsmiths have already proposed fitting remedies (as they humbly conceive), and have, and do offer to take upon them the regulating thereof
as by their answers of the 13th of July last may appear—therefore not
necessary to put the Wire-drawers upon it.

   3rd. They say they are an ancient Corporation, and that the
Common Assay for all Gold and Silver wrought within London and
three miles compass is to be at Goldsmiths Hall, and therefore not

convenient to set up another co-ordinate authority of Assay, lest it produce uncertainty in the manufacture, and contentions among the Companies.

Lastly. The Refiners have ever been Members of the Goldsmiths' Company, and persons very useful to them in their trade for their fincing and parting their gold from silver, and washing their sweeps ; and therefore they may be still continued members of their Company.

As to the particulars of the powers mentioned in their paper, which if thought fit to be thoroughly incorporated, the said Wardens and Assistants then do further humbly offer and pray that the additional clauses hereafter following may be inserted, viz. :—

These suggestions, briefly summarised, were—

That all persons exercising the trade might be translated in the Company of Refiners and Wire-drawers.

That the laws which the Refiners and Wire-drawers might make should not be repugnant to the laws and ordinances of the Goldsmiths, nor a prejudice to their Charters.

That with regard to the clause limiting the right to exercise the trade to those who had served seven years apprenticeship, the service must have been to the said trade or trades of a Goldsmith, viz., such as are now bound apprentices unto Wire-drawers, Free of the Goldsmiths.

That in the paragraph dealing with the right to search, try, assay, and touch their own Manufactures, this clause should be inserted, viz. : " That they be required to assay all and answer the party damaged if " he buys bad assayed, as the Wardens of the Goldsmiths are bound " by Statute, and that the Wardens of the Goldsmiths may supervise " such touch made by the Wire-drawers and punish if defective."

Signed by Order of the Wardens and Assistants of the said Company.

Jo⁺ SPRAKELING, Clerke.

September 23, 1664.

" Which answers being several times read and the same debated, it " was in conclusion put to question, whether it should be presented to " the Council of the Mint as it was now prepared, or not." " And it " was resolved in the affirmative ; " and certain members of the Court were entreated to accompany the Wardens to present the same to the Council as the answers of this Court ; it being subscribed by the Clerk, thus—

"Signed by order of the Wardens and Assistants of the said " Company,

"Jo^N Sprakeling, Clerke."

Owing to the unfortunate gap in the continuity of the Mint Records at this period, the report which the Council was to have made to the King cannot be traced, but that this report was presented in due course is proved by the following extract from the Calendar of State Papers (Domestic series).

November, 1664. "List of Members of Committee to inquire "about Mr. Garrill's new invention, and the Officers of the Mint, Gold- "smiths, and Wyre-Drawers' answers. August 17. 1664."

The terrible calamities which afflicted London during the two following years, viz. the Great Plague in 1665, and the disastrous Fire which nearly destroyed the City in 1666, must have seriously affected the development of the Wyre-Drawing industry; but that it continued to exist, notwithstanding these dreadful calamities, is shown by a document preserved among the State Papers, which mentions the reference to the Attorney-General of a Petition concerning great abuses in making Gold and Silver Lace ; and in 1666 a Bill dealing with the preparing of Gold and Silver Wyre was introduced into the House of Commons. The second reading was, however, refused. *Cal. of State Papers, 1665.*

H. C. Jour- nals, vol. viii. p. 648.

The next allusion to this Trade is found in a Royal Proclamation issued at Edinburgh on March 1, 1680; wherein the exportation of Gold and Silver Thread was forbidden " for the purpose of the increase " of money." *Rüding's Annals of the Coinage.*

From this date down to 1691, when the Gold and Silver Wyre-Drawers made a final and successful effort to obtain their Charter, no further mention can be found of this Society ; but, about this time the House of Commons granted leave to bring in a Bill against wearing Gold and Silver Lace during the war with France. This Bill, how-ever, does not appear to have been proceeded with. *H. C. Jour- nals, vol. xi. p. 364.*

The Gold and Silver Wyre-Drawers had at last passed through the long and wearisome period of their probation, and even " As Gold "shall be tried by Fire," so, it may be assumed, they also emerged from the Furnace of Adversity, tried and purified, and fitted to be numbered with the Incorporated Companies of the City of London.

The story of this Incorporation and their History as a City Company form the subject of the following chapters.

WILLIAM and MARY presenting the CHARTER

CHAPTER VII.

THE Art of Gold and Silver Wyre-Drawing, and of the Spinning of Gold and Silver Thread, etc., having, as will have been seen in the foregoing pages, been long established in England, the efforts of the members of this Trade at last triumphed over all opposition, and finally brought them once again within measurable reach of the summit of their ambition.

The first step which led to the attainment of their desire, was a petition, addressed to the Crown in the third year of the reign of William and Mary, A.D. 1691, by those persons then practising the above-mentioned Trade, Art, and Mystery, in or about the City of London, praying that they might be Incorporated, and that the usual privileges and immunities be granted to them.

This petition having been referred to the Attorney-General, was by him brought before the Court of Aldermen in March, 1691, to obtain their opinion before making his report. The Court of Aldermen referred the petition to a Committee of five of its members, for consideration; with instructions to summon before them the said Wyre-Drawers and whom else might be concerned. *Repertories, V. 95. fol. 229.*

Rep. V. 95,
fol. 246.
Jovis xxv*., die Marti/, 1691.   The Committee delivered their report
to the Court of Aldermen, and which was as follows :—

"Wee are of opinion That such Incorporation will not be pre-
"judiciall to this City, but will be a meanes to regulate many abuses in
"making the Commodities belonging to the said Art, and bring the
"same into greater reputation in forreigne parts, to the advancement
"of Trade and benefitt of the City.   All of which we humbly submitt
"to the grave judgement of this Court"
                    "Signed
                                        "PETER DANIEL
                                        "WM GORE."

Whereupon the Court of Aldermen approved of the Report and
ordered it to be entered in the Repertory; and gave their consent to
the Petitioners to "proceed in theire request to theire Majesties for
"obteyneing letters patents for theire Incorporation."

And the Court further ordered that "Mr. Borrett, the City Solicitor,
"do attend Mr. Attorney General for a Copy of such Letters Patents ;
"to be brought before them for theire perusall and approbation before
"the same doe passe.   And that he desire Mr. Attorney to provide in
"the said Letters Patents that they may not be enabled to take any
"members, though of the same Trade, from any of the Companies of
"this City, without the Licence and Approbation of this Court first had
"and obteyned."

Ibid., fol. 305.
"Marti/ xiiy die July, 1691."

The draft of the Charter of Incorporation, having been perused by
the Recorder, was referred to the previous Committee for their opinion
and report.

Which report was no doubt favourable, for the petition was in
due course acceded to, and on the 16th day of June, A.D. 1693, under
Writ of the Lord Privy Seal (Pigott), the Freemen of the said Trade,
Art, and Mystery were constituted, henceforth and for ever—

"One Body Corporate and Politic in Deed, Fact, and Name ;
"with the title of—Master, Wardens, Assistants, and Commonalty of
"the Art and Mystery of Drawing and Flatting of Gold and Silver
"Wyre ; and—Making and Spinning of Gold and Silver Thread and
"Stuffe in our City of London."

By this Charter of Incorporation many valuable privileges were granted to the Company; amongst others, power was given to make all reasonable Acts, Orders, and Ordinances, with the right to inflict Fines, Pains, and Penalties, in order to enforce them, not only for the good government of the Company, and for the regulation of the Trade Art and Mystery which it represented, but also for the punishment and reformation of such abuses and deceits as might be practised to the detriment of the general welfare of the Trade.

The Company had, in addition, the right to compel the attendance before the Master and Wardens, of all persons engaged in this industry; and to punish those who had served seven years therein for refusing to be made free of the said Company.

This right was largely exercised during the early years of the Company's existence; and the Minute Books of that period bear witness that many persons were summoned to appear before the Master, Wardens, and Assistants for disregarding these regulations; and compliance with them was then enforced.

It will thus be seen that it was compulsory upon all persons engaged in the Trade of Gold and Silver Wyre Drawing, and Spinning of Gold and Silver Thread, to become Members of this Company; and the Master, Wardens, and Assistants were commanded and required to admit to the Company all persons so engaged who were Freemen of the City of London.

It was furthermore provided that no person could practise this industry unless he had served Seven Years at least to a Gold and Silver Wyre-Drawer, or was a duly admitted member of the Company, and subject to its government. In connection with this point it was also ordered that all Apprentices should, at the expiration of the term for which they were bound, be made free of the Company; and their employers were ordered to bind their Apprentices and Servants to, and make them free of this Company only.

Authority was likewise given to the Master, Wardens and Court of Assistants to make Rules with respect to the goodness of Wares; and powers of search, under warrant of the Lord Chief Justice of the Court of King's Bench, were granted, enabling them, with the assistance of a Constable, to make domiciliary visits, and search for and destroy any defective, insufficient, or ill-wrought Wares. Provided always that the exercise of these rights should not extend to the prejudice or diminution of the authorities and privileges theretofore granted of the Goldsmiths' Company.

The Officers of the Company were also made Inspectors of Weights and Measures within the province of the Gold and Silver Wyre-Drawing Trade.

The Company having been created by this Royal Grant, it became necessary, in order to ensure the carrying out of the same, that Officers should be appointed. It was accordingly ordained that Mr. Nathaniel Smith, Citizen, and Gold and Silver Wyre-Drawer, be the first Master of the Company, he previously taking the Oath of allegiance to the King and of fidelity to the Company before the Lord Mayor of the City of London for the time being.

The first Wardens, four in number, were then constituted. They were—Henry Scatcliffe, Thomas Wright, Jacob Sheldrake, and Richard Andrews. And power was given to the first Master to administer the Oath to them.

The number of first Assistants was fixed at Twenty-four; but permission was given to the Master, Wardens, and Assistants to increase the number of the latter to Thirty-six. Each of them having to take his "Corporall Oath" before the Master and Wardens. The first Assistants who were named, constituted, and appointed under the Charter were William Newbery, Thomas Woods, Thomas Jett, Zachary Hickcox, Thomas Bracee, Henry Southhouse, Robert Rhodes, Joseph Tucker, William Wastfield, Francis Smartfoot, William Cousens, John Field, Robert Rouse, Christopher Blower, Joseph Horsley, Job Harris, Samuel Parratt, John Fisher, Samuel Harridge, William Swift, Daniel Biddle, Henry Lovelace, Daniel Field, and Peter Floyer, Alderman (Goldsmith), and afterwards Sheriff; who was Knighted for his services, but died before attaining to the Civic Chair. The Charter also provided and ordered that thirteen members of the Court, of whom the Master or one of the Wardens must be one, should form a Quorum.

This Charter, as briefly summarized in the foregoing passages, was granted as before stated, on the 16th day of June, 1693, in the fifth year of the Reign of William and Mary ; and on the 19th day of September in the same year, it was ordered by the Court of Aldermen "to be inrolled by Mr. Towne Clerke amongst the Records "of this City."

Rep. V. 97, fol. 433.

The expenses attendant upon the obtaining of this Royal Grant were very considerable, amounting to over Six hundred pounds. They appear to have been defrayed by subscriptions collected from the members of the Gold and Silver Wyre-Drawing Trade. No details of this expenditure are, however, shown in the accounts of the Company, the gross amount being simply debited and credited to the account of Mr. Nathaniel Smith, the first Master.

CHAPTER VIII.

HE first Court was held at Guildhall on July 25, 1693, when seven gentlemen were sworn in as Members of the Court of Assistants.

The first Clerk of the Company was a Mr. John Borrett, alluded to, as before mentioned, in the order of the Court of Aldermen, as "the City Solicitor;" and who is described in the earliest account book of the Company as "the Prothonotary who took out its Charter;" and subsequently passed its By-Laws. This gentleman, who appears to have taken the Company under his wing during its infancy, was evidently a man of high position, and, being much occupied with his official duties, he was assisted in the minor work appertaining to the office of Clerk by Mr. Richard Brady, the first Beadle.

This Functionary, then and for many years afterwards, played a much more important part in the affairs of the Company than his successor does at the present time. For, in addition to having to be in attendance upon the Master and Wardens during their periodical visits of inspection to the workshops of the Members of the Trade, and their rounds for the collection of quarterage (then most strictly enforced) he was charged with the duty of serving the numerous summonses issued by the Court of the Company against contumacious and rebellious members, to compel their obedience to its Acts and Ordinances.

By far the greater number of lads who, under the auspices of the Company, were made Apprentices during the first half century of its existence, were bound to the Beadle preparatory to being turned over to their respective Masters. No less than ninety-two Apprentices having in this way been bound to Richard Brady between the years 1693 and 1700; and nearly two hundred to his successor in the Office (George Meakins) during the twenty years ensuing.

Great importance was in these early days attached to the system of Apprenticeship. No less than eight (being one-fifth of the total number) of the Acts and Ordinances relating to this special subject. In some cases large sums of money were given "as consideration" for the privilege of Apprenticeship ; in several instances as much as £240, £260, and even £420, were paid on this account'; and in many others a condition was made that a sum of money should be given to one or other of the City Charities.

The Company during the first hundred years of its rule made no less than One thousand and seventy Apprentices, many of whom were turned over to Members of the various Guilds of the City of London, the remainder serving their time with the Gold and Silver Wyre-Drawers to whom they had been bound.

The Company, being now started and its officers appointed, gradually settled down to its work.

The first entry in the Minute-book duly certifies that Mr. Nathaniel Smith, appointed by their Majesties Letters Patent to be the first Master, attended personally before Sir John Fleet, Kt. and Lord Mayor of the City of London, on the 8th day of July, 1693 ; and took the Oath of Master, mentioned in the Charter.

The next entries set out that, on the 21st and 24th days of the same month, three out of the four gentlemen appointed by the Charter, took the Oaths of Warden, and of fidelity and allegiance, before the Master of the Company ; and, on December 30, 1693, Captain Bracee was elected the fourth Warden, instead of Jacob Sheldrake, who had been nominated by the Charter.

The first business that came before the Court was of considerable interest; it being a petition from the working Wyre-drawers, asking, amongst other things, "That there may always be an equall number of "working Wyer-drawers chosen into the Court of Assistants with the "Stuffe-makers."

The meetings of the Court and the various Committees were, during the first year or two of the Company's career, held at The Plasterers Hall,* in Addle Street, Wood Street; a formal contract for the hire of this Hall having been entered into with the Plasterers Company in 1695.

Shortly afterwards, however, viz. in 1696, the Wyre-Drawers appear to have transferred their favours to the Worshipful Company of Broderers (with which, as with other kindred Guilds, such as the Goldsmiths, Weavers, etc., the new Company seemed at this time to be on very friendly terms); for the accounts for that year show that Rent was then paid for the use of the Broderers Hall.

It is not surprising that the relations of the Gold and Silver Wyre-Drawers with the above-mentioned Companies should, at this time, have been of a friendly, and even intimate description; for, in consequence of the dual nature of the Trade which the Wyre-Drawers were engaged in, many of their members were also free of these older Companies, from which, indeed, it may be asserted, the Wyre-Drawers were an off-shoot.

On December 30, 1693, that being the regular date for the election of officers, the Court re-elected Mr. Nathaniel Smith as Master; and continued the three first Wardens in their Offices. Mr. Borrett was also at this meeting chosen Clerk of the Company.

About this date it was ordered that the General Courts be held monthly; and that the Committees meet every fortnight. The Company also purchased the "Escritoire," which is constantly alluded to in the Minute books during the ensuing one hundred years.

The time and attention of the Court appear, however, to have been mainly taken up, for the first few years, with the consideration of the Acts, Orders, and Ordinances, which, indeed, were not finally drafted and approved before January, 1700.

To this, one important exception must be made, for in January,

* The Company first met at this Hall in October, 1693.

1697/8 (Old Style), the Court took into serious consideration the question of the importation of Foreign Lace, and resolved itself into a Grand Committee to attend Parliament *re* the affairs of the Company.

Sir Henry Hobart, M.P., was interviewed with reference to a Bill to be brought into the House of Commons, and the Court shortly afterwards drafted the heads of the Clauses of the Bill, which eventually became Law, and is subsequently often alluded to as " The Wyre-Drawers Act." 9 William III. c. 39 (1698), British Museum, large fol. Stat. and Acts.

The Committee having had a difference with Sir Henry Hobart, appealed to Sir Robert Davers, M.P., who took up the matter of their Bill. The duration of this Act was limited to three years, but on its expiration it was renewed for a further period of seven years. 1. Anne, cap. xi., British Museum, large fol. Stat. and Acts.

These two Acts are fully described in the Appendix, it is therefore sufficient to state here that they were of very great importance to the Company, inasmuch as they settled the proportion of Silver and Silk to be used in the making of Gold and Silver Thread ; prohibited the spinning of Copper, Brass, or other inferior metal upon Silk ; and also forbade the importation of Gold and Silver Thread, Lace, Fringe, or other work made thereof, and of Thread or work made of Copper or other inferior metal, into the Kingdom of England; the dominion of Wales ; or Town of Berwick on Tweed ; under pain of being forfeited and burnt.

The second Act provided that a penalty of £100, in addition to the previous forfeiture and burning, should be paid by the Importer. 1. Anne, cap. xi.

This penalty, as will be seen later on, was included in subsequent Acts, and was several times proceeded for and recovered by the Company.

About this time, viz. 1698, the Copper Wire-Drawers are shown by an entry in the account book to have paid the Company the sum of Thirty Pounds.

The cost of obtaining this first Act of Parliament, as well as the expenses attending the passing of the By Laws (or Acts and Ordinances,) were, as with the Charter, paid from subscriptions contributed by Members of the Trade and Company.

In December, 1698, the Master and Wardens appear for the first time to have applied for and obtained from Sir Elathiell Lovell,

Recorder of the City of London, a warrant empowering them to search for ill-made and insufficient goods; and early in the following year the Court unanimously resolved that persons found guilty of making insufficient goods should be prosecuted; and agreed to defend any action brought against any Member of the Court for cutting and destroying such goods.

Appended is a Fac-simile copy of the Account of the Expenditure of the Company during the first year of its existence.

Anno
1694   Contr⟩ C⟨

May 22 Paid for the Act of Parliam' For Duties upon Paper &c   00 01 00
     25 Paid for another Act Relating to the Orphans — — —   00 01 00
         For Covering 4 Bookes in Marbled Paper — — — — —   00 00 06
         For 3 Quire of Paper and a Botle of Ink — — — —   00 02 03
June 8.&15 For Coffee &c at the Hall — — — — — —   00 00 10
         Ditto Expended at the Grecian Coffee house w'th Warden⟩
            Biddle Mr Lovelace and Mr Barrett — — — —⟨   00 01 02
         Ditto Paid for an Abstract of the Paper Act — — —   00 00 03
      Do For Coach hire from the Temple — — — —   00 01 00
      18 Paid to the Town Clerk for an Order to make 14 free   05 12 00
      27 Expended at Gild Hall Coffee house with the Wardens   00 00 05
      Do Expended at the Devill Tavern p Temple Barr —   00 05 00
      Dr For Coach hire to the Temple and back again — —   00 02 00
July 6 Given (p order) to Mr Denison's Maid — — — —   00 02 06
      Do Paid for an Hour glass — — — — — —   00 00 08
      12 Paid for Stamping 12 pair of Indentures — —   00 12 00
      20 Paid for Ale and Beere and Reysins at the Hall —   00 00 05
      25 Paid at the Hen and Chickens in Wood Street at a⟩
            meeting with the Plaister Company — — —⟨   00 01 00
Augt 3 For Coffee &c at the Hall — — — — —   00 00 04½
         Paid a Quarters Rent for the Hall Due at Midsom —   02 00 00
Sep 10 Paid at Mr Kittle's at the Auditing the Mast's Accomp — 00 00 11
      14 Paid Mr Warden Wright 7 Guinias Value — — —   07 14 00
      21 Paid for a Quart of Coffee and 3 Faggotts at the Hall 00 01 03½
            Rest to Ballance this Acco.t — — — —   19 10 05
                                                                ————————
                                                                 36 11 00

         This Account was Audited on Fryday —
         the 26th day of October 1694 ⟨p⟩ —

CHAPTER IX.

H E Court, after much deliberation, finally settled and approved the above-mentioned Acts and Ordinances (or By Laws as they were then termed), at a "full Court," held on the 19th day of January, 1699 (Old Style) or as it would now be written, 1700, and, in conformity with an Act of Parliament passed in the 19th year of the Reign of King Henry VII., prohibiting all Masters, Wardens, and Fellowships of Crafts and Mysteries, and all Rulers of Guilds and Fraternities, under a penalty of £40 for each offence, from making or executing any Acts and Ordinances in diminution of the King's prerogative, or against the common profit of the People, unless the same shall have been duly examined and approved by the Lord Chancellor of England, or Chief Justice of either Bench, or three of them ;—the Master, Wardens, and Court of Assistants duly addressed a petition to Sir Nathan Wright, Lord Keeper of the Great Seal, praying him to refer their Book of Acts, Orders, Ordinances, and Oaths unto the two Lord Chief Justices for perusal and amendment, as they might see fit.

Sir Nathan Wright having (on the 15th August, 1700,) complied with the prayer of the petitioners, the Acts, Orders, Ordinances, and Oaths were on the 17th Day of October, A.D. 1700, duly ratified and allowed under the Seals of the Lord Chancellor ; Sir John Holt, Chief Justice of the Court of King's Bench ; and Sir George Treby, Chief Justice of the Court of Common Pleas.

These Acts and Ordinances, some thirty-nine in number, ordain, amongst other provisions, that Four Quarterly Courts shall be held, and fix the dates upon which such meetings shall take place ; and furthermore settle the amount of the Fine for non-attendance by any Member of the Company who shall be summoned thereto.

The date for the Election of Master and Wardens is also indicated, and the duration of their term of Office is fixed ; a Fine of Ten Pounds is moreover to be imposed upon any person who shall refuse to take upon himself either of the said offices.

The Fine for refusal to serve the office of Assistant to the Company is fixed at Twenty Pounds ; and for non-attendance at the Meetings of the Court at Two shillings and sixpence.

The Renter Warden is required to give a Bond for Five hundred Pounds, as security, before taking up this office.

Three Auditors must be appointed every year ; who shall within two months after the election of the New Master and Wardens, examine, inspect, and audit the Accounts of their predecessors.

The Master and Wardens, or any three of them, may meet together at any time to bind Apprentices to Members of the Company, and make free of the Company such persons as shall have served their Apprenticeship, or otherwise have a right to be made free of the Company.

Certain provisions were also made in the event of a Livery being granted to the Company ; fixing the Fee for admission thereto at the sum of Ten Pounds, and the Fine for refusing to take up the Livery at the sum of Twenty Pounds.

The Court, even at this early date, was not unmindful of the rites and duties of Hospitality ; and for the due observance of the same it enacted that " The Master, Wardens, and Court of Assistants should " every year, yearly, Elect and Choose three or more persons, Members " of the said Company, to be Stewards.   And who shall for the Honor " of this Honorable City and the said Company, find and provide, at " their own mutual and equal costs and charges, Two such competent

A Bill of Fare 1721

Three Dishes of Boild Fowles 3 in a Dish with Oyster Sauce & forst meal Balls

Three Dishes of Turkeys & Chines a Turkey & Chine each in a Dish

Three Dishes of Geese, two in each Dish with apple Sauce

Three Dishes of Tongue & Udder a Tongue & Udder in each Dish & a plate of Sausage

Three Dishes of Wild Ducks Four in each Dish with Onion & gravy sauce

Three Marrow Puddings

Three Apple Pyes

Three Dishes of Mince Pyes Six in a Dish

Three Stands of Fruite

" Feasts and Dinners as the Master and Wardens of the said Company
" for the time being shall direct and appoint. One to be called the
" Steward's Dinner, and to be held always on Lord Mayor's Day ; the
" other, to be termed the Election Dinner or Feast, and to be held on
" the day of Election of every new Master and Wardens."

And to ensure the due fulfilment of this obligation, a Fine of
Fifteen Pounds was to be imposed for refusing to serve the Office of
Steward.

Notwithstanding which penalty, much trouble ensued with certain
members of the Company, who failed to see this question of Hospitality,
exercised at their expense, in quite the same light in which it was
regarded by those who were to partake thereof.

Some pleaded poverty, and were consequently excused ; others flatly
refused to carry out the duties of the position, and had to be constrained thereto by threats to issue a Writ, and in several instances by
the actual serving upon them of the Writ in the action for the recovery
of the Penalty.

The Court also, in order to guard against undue regard for economy
on the part of the Stewards, provided a set Bill of Fare which did duty
for the Years 1721 to 1731 inclusive, and a copy of which is appended.

With a view to defraying the necessary expenses of the Company,
it was ordained that every member thereof should contribute the sum
of two shillings yearly, as Quarterage money, payable by quarterly
instalments of sixpence ; and for that purpose should attend each
Quarter Court day to pay the same to the Renter Warden.

In practice, however, it was very quickly found that this regulation
would not work.   Members soon got several, and in a great number of
instances, many quarters in arrears ; and it consequently became
necessary to make arrangements for the personal collection of Quarterage.   To which purpose the City of London and Borough of Southwark were mapped out into districts, each to be worked by the Master,
or one of the Wardens, assisted by several members of the Court, and
by the Beadle of the Company.

These various posses of Collectors were wont to assemble at
certain Coffee Houses, between seven and eight o'clock in the morning,
previous to starting upon their rounds ; and first arranging a place of

meeting for the afternoon, there to count up their takings, and refresh themselves after the arduous duties they had so painstakingly performed.

Members of the Company were also made liable to contribute their proportion, in common with other members, "of all Charges, Scots, "Lots, Sume or Sumes of money, Taxes, and Tallages, that might be "assessed and imposed upon them, not only for the necessary affairs "and honour of the City, and for the welfare and good estate of the "Company, but also for the provision of Corn and Grain for the supply "of the Poor, according to Ancient Custom."

The clauses in the Acts and Ordinances relating to Apprentices may be briefly summarised as follows :—

No member of the Company, or person exercising the Art or Trade of Drawing and Flatting of Gold and Silver Wyre, or of Spinning or Makeing of Thread or Stuffs, shall be "capable" to take an "Apprentice "until he have been a Freeman of the City of London for at least two "years; under a penalty of Five Pounds."

He also shall not take a second Apprentice before his first shall have served three years and a half of his time ; the penalty for disregarding this regulation being a Fine of Ten Pounds payable to the Master and Wardens. And any such person taking or keeping more than two Apprentices at any one time, shall pay a Fine of Forty Shillings per month for each and every Apprentice kept in excess of the number provided for.

No apprentice was allowed to be kept longer than one month on trial before being bound by Indentures before the Master and Wardens, and duly registered in the Book kept by the Clerk of the Company.

The fees for the binding of Apprentices were settled, and provision was made for their enrollment at the Chamberlain's Office, within twelve months of their being bound ; the Fine for non compliance with this ordinance being fixed at Six shillings and eightpence.

Any member of the Company who should have one or more Apprentices bound to him by a Scrivener, or other person whatsoever than by the Clerk of the Company, was liable to a penalty of Five Pounds.

Apprentices could not be assigned, turned over, or put away, without the consent of the Master and Wardens. And in the events of the death of their employer (Master) the Master and Wardens had power to assign such Appprentices who had not served their full time, to any person or persons whom they in their discretion might think fit.

Every Apprentice, upon the completion of his Indentures, was, within Forty days of the expiration thereof, to be brought by his Master before the Court of Assistants, and if his conduct and service had been true and faithful, he was then to be made free of the Company.

No member of the Company was allowed to teach the Trade of Drawing and Flatting of Gold and Silver Wyre, etc., to any person other than his Apprentice, or to his wife or child; nor even work with any one not free of the Company, under a penalty of Twenty-five pounds.

It was also ordained that no person within the Cities of London and Westminster, the suburbs thereof, or within Thirty miles distance, should practise the said Trade, Art, and Mystery, unless he had served seven years to, or had been instructed in the Trade, or had been examined by the Court of Assistants, and made free of the Company; under a penalty of Five Pounds, and further Fine of Forty Shillings per month for continuing in his offence.

Widows were, however, allowed to pursue the Trade of their deceased husband, during widowhood, after having been made free of the Company.

No Journeyman was permitted to be employed by any member of the Company unless he (the journeyman) were free of it.

No member of the Company could arrest or sue another member, relative to any matter concerning the Trade, without first acquainting the Master and Wardens with the subject of the dispute. " To the end " that all differences arising between members of the same Company " might be friendly compromised by the good discretion of the Master " and Wardens, with their Assistants, if need be, and Brotherly Peace " by that means be preserved."

The Master, Wardens, and Assistants had power to remove any Officer or member of the Livery of the Company from his office, if found guilty of any crime in relation to the Trade, and therefore deemed by them unworthy of place or office, or other esteem in the said company, and could also restore the offender to his former dignity after submission and reformation.

In order to prevent Fraud and Deceit in the Trade, the Master, Wardens, and Assistants were empowered to make rules for the goodness of Gold and Silver Wares, and for the Spinning of Brass and Copper, and other inferior Metals ; and could impose a Fine not exceeding Ten pounds for non-observance of these Rules.

Gauges were also to be kept at the Hall of the Company, or other convenient place, for the sizing of " Wyre," and all persons engaged in the Trade were required to repair to the said size from time to time, to prove and try by these gauges, their Gold and Silver Wyre.

A penalty of Five pounds was likewise to be inflicted upon any person engaged in this Trade who should improperly spin Gold and Silver plate or thread, in any other manner than that provided for by the regulations, and sanctioned by the custom of the Trade.

It was further ordered and ordained, that the Master, Wardens, and Assistants, or any five of them, whereof the Master or one of the Wardens was to be one, should and might, so often as they thought fit and needful, make search, view, and assay all goods and wares used in the said Trade, in order to find out, reform, regulate, and punish all frauds, deceits, and abuses. And in such search to enter the Houses, Shops, or Warehouses of all persons using the said trade, and also in such search to try all weights, beams, and scales used for weighing the said goods and wares ; and if they found insufficient or ill-wrought goods, or deceitful or bad weights and scales, the person in whose possession they were was liable to a Fine not exceeding Five Pounds for each offence. And if any person should resist the Master, Wardens, and Assistants in their search, or refuse to obey them, he was to be fined Ten Pounds for such opposition.

All freemen of the Company were required to be of good will and behaviour, to honestly and well demean themselves, and to be tractable and obedient to all the lawful orders and ordinances of the Company.

In default of due payment of any of the aforesaid Fines and Penalties, the Master, Wardens, Assistants, and Commonalty had power to recover the same by Action for Debt in any of his Majesty's

Courts of Record, or levy the same by Distress by the Beadle, or any other officer of the Company, on the Goods and Chattels of the person or persons chargeable with the said penalties.

Finally, the Court of Assistants had discretionary power to lessen, remit, and discharge any of the Fines, Forfeitures, and Penalties as it might think fit.

The Oaths to be taken by the Master, Wardens, Assistants, Clerk, and Beadle were also included in the Book of Acts, Ordinances, etc., ratified and allowed by the Lord Chancellor and the two Chief Justices.

The Court of Assistants, on being informed by Counsel that it had sufficient power to prosecute any member, either of the Company or Trade, for doing contrary to any of the ordinances mentioned in the By-Laws, resolved to proceed against any such offender with the utmost rigour.

CHAPTER X.

HIS period of time, viz. from the date when the Acts and Ordinances, and the first Act of Parliament were obtained, down to the granting of a Livery, is marked by the great activity displayed by the Company; which, having had an important charge laid upon it, and being entrusted with full powers for the due carrying out of the same, applied itself steadfastly, and with great single-mindedness, to the strict performance of the duty imposed upon it. And if the methods employed do not altogether commend themselves to the free-trade views of modern days, regard must be had, not only to the circumstances of the time, and the customs of Trade then prevalent, but also to the nature of the task which the Company was called upon to perform; namely, the reducing into good order and governance of an industry which, although long-established in the Country, had experienced so many vicissitudes of fortune, that it had fallen into a very disorganized state; a task, moreover, which, on account of the number of persons engaged in the Trade, must have been far from easy to carry out; for in a petition addressed to Parliament in 1743, by the Overseers of the Poor, Churchwardens, Vestries, and Freeholders of the Parishes of St. Giles

House of
Commons
Journals, vol.
xxiv. pp. 397
and 398.

Cripplegate, and St. Luke's, against a Bill recently brought in, by which it was proposed to prohibit the wearing of Gold and Silver Lace, Thread, or Wire in Apparel, it was stated " That in the said Parishes " were upwards of Six thousand persons (including women and children) "engaged in the Trade.   That the poor-rate was already Three " Shillings in the £ ; and that if the Bill became Law all these persons " would be reduced to destitution and become an unsupportable burden "upon the Rates."

It also appears from the Quarterage books of the period that, in 1715, there were no less than Three hundred and fifty-eight persons, principally Master men, who, as members of the Company, were contributing to its support by this means.

One of the greatest drawbacks with which the Company had to contend was, however, its poverty—a state of things which seems to have come about partly owing to the fact that the majority of its members were, unfortunately, not men of substance ; and partly in consequence of the very large expenditure to which the Company was committed from time to time, in connection with the various Bills which it promoted and carried through Parliament (and also those which it opposed as being detrimental to the interests of the Gold and Silver Wyre-Drawing Trade), as well as by reason of the many law-suits in which it became involved, owing to the strict performance of the semi-official duties of search, inspection, and seizure devolving upon it.

As an illustration of the Company's position in these matters, the following extract from the Minutes may be of interest : "June 12, 1701. " An officer of the Customs attended to report the seizure of ill-wrought "wares, directed to a Merchant."   " The Court appointed a Committee "of the Master and Wardens to attend and speak with the Commis- " sioners of Customs at the examination of this Merchant."

Another illustration of the powers exercised by the Company occurs in the Minutes of the same date, viz. " John Hughes, Gold- "smith, made submission, and paid the charge of his Arrest for " denying search ; whereupon the Committee of the Court with- " drew the proceedings and admitted him to the Freedom of the " Company."

On this same date is also found an entry recording that the Court ordered three thousand summonses to be printed.   This shows the resolute way in which the By Laws were being enforced.

The lack of Funds, above alluded to, appears to have been characteristic of the Gold and Silver Wyre-Drawers Company down almost to the present time ; and, repeatedly in the past, subscriptions had to be invited from its members, and others interested in the Trade, in order to clear off the heavy charges, amounting in several instances to nearly Two hundred pounds, for Parliamentary and legal proceedings in connection with its Acts and Ordinances.   Indeed the principal, if not the only omission which the Gold and Silver Wyre-Drawers of the present day have to reproach their predecessors with, consists in the want of foresight which prevented them from then making, at a trifling outlay, those judicious investments which have placed so many of the City Companies in their present fortunate and prosperous condition.   It is probably due to the aforesaid want of means experienced by the earlier Members of the Guild, that so few legacies have been willed to the Company.

The first mentioned was one of Ten Pounds, left in 1713 by Christopher Blower, a very popular member of the Court, and who for two successive years ably occupied the Master's Chair.   By his will this sum was to be spent in the purchase of a Silver Tankard, which was done, and the piece of plate, a fine specimen of " Queen Anne " work, was duly engraved with an inscription and the donor's Arms,— and is now in the possession of the Company.

The next bequest to the Company was that of One hundred pounds, made by Matthew Abbot, a member of the Court, in 1735.

Another, of Forty pounds, was made by Mr. John Court, in 1758 ; and in 1763, an entry in the Account Book sets out that £100 Stock was transferred from Mrs. Berkeley, probably the widow of Robert Berkeley, who was Master in 1741.

There was also the sum of £100 (together with a small Silver Salver), left in 1723 by will of Mrs. Christian Russell, widow, " to " Trustees upon trust, to pay yearly, for ever, Five Pounds on New " Years Day, viz. Twenty shillings a piece, to Five poor widows whose " husbands were free of this Company."

The Minute-book of the proceedings of the Court of Assistants shows that the Trustees of the Will paid over the above-mentioned sum of £100 to the Master and Wardens, who duly invested it (with other sums) in Stock; and the interest accruing upon the same has, down to the present day, been regularly divided, as directed by the terms of the Will, amongst the distressed widows of Freemen of the Company.

This Charity is the only one which has been left to the Gold and Silver Wyre-Drawers Company to administer; yet, notwithstanding the paucity of funds placed at their disposal for Charitable purposes, the members have never been unmindful of this most excellent virtue. Indeed, the records of the Company bear frequent witness that when Members of the Court were found to be in reduced circumstances, part, and in some cases the whole, of their Fine, as Assistant, was returned to them, as were also sums of money which in more prosperous days they had advanced for the necessities of the Company.

As an illustration of this, one member of the Court in 1741 being "in very poor circumstances and then in the Fleet Prison," made an appeal to the Company for the return of part of his Fine, which was at once acceded to.

Owing to the fact that so many women and girls have been, and still are, employed in the manufacture of Gold and Silver Lace, the Company has been brought into relationship with "the weaker sex;" and it is a very pleasing feature of the Company's record that it has ever been mindful of their interests, having from the very first admitted them, when widows, to its freedom; thus enabling them to continue their husbands' business.

This was done in the case of Mrs. Christian Russell, who, in 1716, received the permission of the Court to carry on her late husband's trade; and who, seven years later, showed her appreciation of this solicitude for her welfare, by the Charity of £100, which she left to the Company to administer. This lady's virtues are duly recorded on a Mural tablet in the wall of St. Alphage's Church in London Wall.

The first widow admitted was Mrs. Sarah Cranfield, who was made free of the Company in April, 1701; and the minute-book shows that in the following month two more ladies were likewise made members of the Company. The System of Apprenticeship was also thrown open to females; for in May, 1712, the books record that "Bridget Blake, "daughter of Richard Blake, was bound Apprentice for Seven Years."

It is, furthermore, worthy of note that the field of merit has at all times been open to Industry; for the Minute books and Registers bear frequent witness how often Apprentices, who in due course became free of the Company, eventually rose to the high position of Master.

And it is of equal interest to observe how frequently contumacious Wyre-Drawers, who at first strongly resisted the action taken against them by the Company, after being constrained to submission, joined it, and later on made most excellent Masters. A notable instance of this is seen in the case of a certain Mr. Washburne, who, having had legal proceedings taken against him for denying search, etc., afterwards became reconciled to the Company; and the minute-book shows that both in 1728 and 1729 either he or his son occupied the Master's chair.

In 1703 a point of much interest, in relation to Quarterage, came before the Court. The Master, in consequence of the low state of the Company's funds at the time, proposing, "That if every member of the "Court would advance Twenty shillings, they should be excused from "paying Quarterage for ever, or for so many years as the Court should "think fit." And it was also proposed, "That any person who should "be called upon the Court of Assistants, might elect to pay a Fine of "Twenty shillings in order to discharge himself from paying any "Quarterage."

The consideration of this matter was deferred; but in February of the following year, the Committee having first reported in favour of the suggestion, the Court, by resolution, adopted this proposal for the Commutation of Quarterage, and many members, then and subsequently, took advantage of the opportunity to release themselves from an irksome little liability.

The Gold and Silver Wyre-Drawers appear to have been very constant to the various places at which they were in the habit of meeting, and made as few changes as possible. Having, in 1696, found a home at the Broderer's ("Embroyderers") Hall, they settled down there for thirteen years, and only then left, viz. in 1709, for reasons of economy; the rent being found to be a great burden on the Company.

The Court, therefore, resolved to migrate to Bracy's Coffee House in Silver Street, where its meetings were held until 1714, when a change was made to Tom's Coffee House in Wood Street. This change was evidently a very satisfactory one, for the Court continued to meet there during the ensuing twenty-seven years, viz. down to 1741, when, in consequence of the death of the proprietor, the Court decided to find fresh quarters at the Half Moon Tavern in Cheapside ; to which hostelry it remained faithful until beyond the period of time dealt with in this Chapter.

The Company, even so far back as 1702, appears to have met with the same inconvenience arising from the non-attendance of Members of the Court, as is sometimes experienced at the present day ; but in those times men seemed either to take a more practical view of this matter, or were less governed by sentiment and excess of good nature ; for it is recorded in that year, " That the Clerk was ordered to write to "several members of the Court, desiring them to state in writing "whether they were willing to attend the Courts, or be dismissed and "let others be elected in their place." Whereupon Mr. Robert Rhodes resigned his position on the Court of Assistants by letter, as follows : " I desire the Master and the rest of your Court that they will be "pleased to elect another in my Room for I cannot give my Attendance, "being my occasions lyes so far off ; otherwise should be glad to do all "the Service that lay in my Power ; wishing you and them all Happi- "ness in your undertakings.   I am, etc.

" (Signed)   ROBERT RHODES."

In June, 1702, a Committee of the Court resolved, " That the " Master and Wardens do wait on Mr. Chamberlain to have his opinion "whether the Company might, without prejudice to itself, admit into its "Freedom the Lacemen, Copper Wire-Drawers, etc.," and in the following month the Master reported to the Court, " that he had been "referred by the Chamberlain to, Mr. Dee, the Common Sergeant, for his opinion on this matter."

Whereupon the Court resolved, " That the Master, Wardens, and "several of the Assistants be a Committee to draw up some questions "to ask Mr. Dee about admitting into the Freedom of this Company, "the Copper Wire-Drawers, Lacemen, and Weavers."

Nothing, however, appears to have resulted from this action, but about this time many Goldsmiths joined the Company, and gave it considerable support; their apprentices were also, at the expiration of their time, made free of this Company by Redemption ; and in connec- tion with this matter an order was received from the Court of Aldermen, granting the petition of the Company " that all persons who had served " their time to any Freeman of the City, using the trade of a Gold and " Silver Wyre-Drawer, should although bound to other Companies, be " admitted to the Freedom of this Company by Redemption."

The Acts of Parliament relating to the manufacture of Gold and Silver Lace, and the steps taken by the Court of Assistants to obtain the same, form a most interesting part of the annals of the Company ; as showing the great efforts that were being made to foster this im- portant industry.

The first Act has already been alluded to, and with regard to the second, which practically renews the former one, the Company appears to have been aroused to action by the report " that the Lacemen were " applying to Parliament to have the Gold and Silver Wyre-Drawers " Act revived, and to get an Act to ' Impower' (? Incorporate) them- " selves."

1 Anne, cap. xi.

The Court accordingly resolved that a Committee should attend at Parliament, to ascertain what measures might be taken about the said Act on behalf of the Company ; and two days later, viz. on January 26, 1702, the Court decided that the Company's Act should be continued, " and the said Act was then read over paragraph by paragraph, and " several amendments agreed to."   The whole Court then formed itself into a Committee to carry the matter through, and resolved that, " In " order to defray the necessary charges, each member do lend two " guineas to the Company."   The Court also decided to take the Charter and By Laws to the House of Commons for consultation with the members.

On the 15th of May, in the same year, the new Act was " read " over, and very well approved of ; " and it was then ordered to be advertised in the *Gazette*, in the Company's name, " that no person " might plead ignorance."

The Court is next seen (in October, 1702) to be considering the question of approaching the Civic Parliament, with a view of obtaining an Act of Common Council; and appointed a Committee for this purpose. After much deliberation, a Bill appears to have been drafted; for in March, 1703, the Clerk reported the opinion of the Common Sergeant thereon; which was as follows :—

" That the Company had power by the Custom of the City to enter " in the day time, any person's shop who exercises the Trade (the door " being open), and may there and then, view the workmanship of such " person's wares and goods; and if the Company should find upon " such their search and view, any wares and goods deceitfully and " badly wrought and made, they may seize and bring the same to " Guildhall, and there upon a Jury's Inquest (the person whose wares " and goods so seized being Summoned to appear before the Jury) to " inquire if the same are well wrought and made; and if the Jury finds " the same not to be well wrought or made, then the Company may, by " the same power, presently burn the same in Guildhall Yard."

This opinion was evidently accepted as decisive, for no further mention is made of " the Act of Common Council."

The next Act of Parliament (known as a Revenue Act) was viewed 10 Anne, with strong disfavour by the Company, as being, in its opinion, very cap. 19, secs. 48-68. detrimental to the Gold and Silver Wyre-Drawers. The Court therefore appointed the Master and Wardens a Committee to endeavour to prevent Duty being laid upon Gold and Silver Wyre.

These efforts were, however, unsuccessful, for the Bill, which imposed a Duty of One shilling per ounce on all Gilt wire, and ninepence per ounce on all Silver wire, imported into the Kingdom of Great Britain, and also imposed a Duty of Eightpence per ounce on all Gilt wire, and of sixpence per ounce upon all Silver wire, made in Great Britain, became law, and was made operative for thirty-two years.

Very strict regulations were ordained, and heavy penalties provided against non-compliance with the Clauses of this Act dealing with the entries and returns to be made by Wyre-Drawers.

The last section, however, enacted that, during the continuance of the said Duties upon Gold and Silver Wyre, granted by this Act, no Gold and Silver Thread, Lace, Fringe or other work made thereof

G

should be imported into Great Britain upon pain of being forfeited, and upon the further penalty of a Fine of One hundred pounds.

Not discouraged by their previous failures, the Members of the Court, in the following year, viz. 171¾, made another gallant attempt to get the obnoxious Duties repealed. A Committee was appointed for this purpose, who interviewed several members of Parliament, and were by them encouraged to petition the House of Commons, and to try and obtain a drawback. This was done, and the petition was referred to a Committee of the House ; but there the matter appears to have ended.

The attention of the Company was next drawn to Parliamentary business in 1720, in connection with a recent Act relating to the Duty on Plate; the question being whether Gold and Silver Wyre was chargeable. A Committee was appointed to confer with the Commissioners of Excise, and the Court resolved to employ the Clerk of the Goldsmiths Company to draw up a Case. Counsel's opinion was subsequently taken, and a decision of the Commissioners eventually obtained. " That the Company should not be charged with Duty "other than that mentioned in the Gold and Silver Wyre-Drawers Act "of Parliament."

This must refer to the Revenue Act of 10 Anne, Cap. 19, the previous Acts, which, moreover, did not mention " Duty," having long since expired.

In 1731, the Court resolved to draw up a petition to the King and Council against a Bill expected to be transmitted from Ireland, and which it was supposed would prove detrimental to the Trade of the Company. No further mention is however made of this.

The Company appears to have remained quiet during the ensuing ten years; viz. until 1741, when it took into its consideration the question of the Act of Parliament, prohibiting the working of Copper wire and plate on silk, having expired ; and decided to endeavour to get it renewed : but being advised that such action would be improper, on account of the great lapse of time since the expiration of the old Act, the Court resolved to try and obtain a fresh one—and the Master, Wardens, and Committee of the Assistants waited on the Speaker of the House of Commons in this matter, who referred them to the

Commissioners of Excise; and these Gentlemen were petitioned accordingly.

In the following year the Court again considered this question, supplemented by that of the Importation of Foreign Lace.

A Committee was nominated, and the powerful aid of the Lord Mayor obtained to present their petition to the House of Commons. *Either George Heathcote or Sir Robert Godschall, both M.P's.*

The record now passes from the Minute-book of the Company to the Journals of the House of Commons, where most valuable and interesting information is found.

The first entry of importance is on March 15, 174½, and sets out that the petition "of Manufacturers of Gold and Silver Wyre against "the importation of Counterfeit Lace," was presented to the House. *II. C. J. xxiv. 15 Geo. II. p. 122.* This petition recited the previous Acts, and stated that, " Owing to " the expiration of the last of which some Thirty years previously, large " quantities of Tinsel, Copper, and other base metal had been brought " into the Kingdom partly manufactured, and was then spun upon Silk, " and worked up in imitation of Gold and Silver Lace, to the Dis- " couragement of that Trade in particular, and of the most dangerous " consequence to the Public in General." The Petition was referred to a Committee consisting of the Lord Mayor and all the Merchants of the House.

In the following month this Committee reported in favour of the Petition, and adduced evidence proving the importation of the baser metals from Nuremberg, and quoted the price as being little more than as many pence as the real article was shillings. *Ibid., p. 168.*

Leave was accordingly given to bring in a Bill to prevent these frauds; and "that the Lord Mayor and Sir John Barnard do prepare " and bring in the same." An Instruction was also given to the Com- mittee that they insert in the Bill certain similar clauses to those in the previous Acts relating to the proper proportions of Silver and of Silk, etc.

The Lord Mayor brought in the Bill, which passed through its successive stages, and he then, by order, took it up to the House of Lords. This Bill duly passed the House of Lords, and received the Royal Assent in June, 1742. *Ibid., p. 170. II. L. J. xxvi. p. 144.*

The Act, which was made a Public one, was to take effect from

July 1, 1742; and no limit to its duration was fixed. Briefly described, it renewed the previous Acts, and provided the same penalties, and in addition, to ensure the quality of the Metal, it enacted that the Ingot of Silver, before the Gold was applied, should be weighed in the presence of an Officer of Excise, and again after the gilding process had been effected, to prove that the due amount of Fine Gold, viz. 4 dwt. 4 grns. per pound weight (Troy) of Silver, had been put on.   A penalty of Twenty pounds being provided in case of refusal to admit the Officer.

Material, made from Copper, etc., to be used in Theatrical Performances, was, however, specially exempted from the provisions of this Act.

The account of the Company's Solicitor for obtaining this Act amounted to £185, and a further sum of Twenty Pounds was voted to him as a Gratuity.

The Court of Assistants at once began to enforce this Act; and, as a preliminary, approved Advertisements to be inserted in the papers; and ordered Two thousand copies of them to be dispersed about the Town.

A most serious crisis in the history of the Company, threatening, not only its own existence, but also that of the Industry which the Company represented, was reached in 1743.

H. C. J. xxiv.   In that year three Members of Parliament, to wit, Lord Strange,
p. 379.   Mr. Gibbon, and Mr. Sydenham, obtained Leave of the House to bring in a Bill " prohibiting the wearing of Gold and Silver Lace,
Ibid., p. 388.   "Thread, or Wire, in Apparel;" and on the 24th of January, this Bill was brought in by Lord Strange and read the first time.

Directly the Members of the Worshipful Company of Gold and Silver Wyre-Drawers heard of this threatening attack upon their interests, they realized the vital nature of the struggle that was before them, and set to work manfully to oppose the Bill before Parliament. Subscriptions were invited from the Members of the Trade, and the assistance of the Members for the City was invoked.

The Weavers Company at this juncture gallantly came forward to the assistance of the Wyre-Drawers, and appointed a Committee to confer with them in this matter; they also collected subscriptions, amounting to fifty pounds, towards the cost of opposing the Bill; which sum they paid over to Mr. Turner, a member of the Court of the Gold and Silver Wyre-Drawers Company, and Mr. Turner was instructed to confer with Lord Duplin in regard to this opposition.

The scene of the contest was then shifted to the House of Commons; the first step in the defence being the reading of the Company's petition, which represented "That if the Bill passed, not "only themselves, but some thousands of families would be reduced to "want and great necessity." H. C. J. xxiv. p. 395.

This petition was ordered to lie upon the Table, and leave was given to the Petitioners to be heard by Counsel.

Further petitions against the Bill from the Dealers in Gold and Silver Lace, Weavers, and Fringe-Makers were immediately afterwards presented, shortly followed by the one (previously alluded to) from the Churchwardens and Overseers of the Parishes of St. Luke and St. Giles, Cripplegate. Ibid., pp. 397, 398.

The Bailiff, Wardens, and Assistants of the Weavers Company next brought forward their petition against the proposed legislation; and to them succeeded the Manufacturers of Gold and Silver Wyre in the City of Coventry, and the Mayor, Bailiffs, and Commonalty of that City; all protesting and petitioning against this wanton interference with their Trade. Ibid., p. 399. Ibid., p. 404.

So much opposition was not without its due effect upon the House of Commons, who accordingly declined to read the Bill a second time on the following Monday (as previously set down), and ordered it to be read that day Two Months (equivalent to "This day Six months"), i.e. dropped. Ibid., p. 412.

This signal victory put fresh heart into the Company, which immediately set about its work with renewed vigour, and at once passed a resolution to prosecute all persons dealing in Copper Lace; first, however, paying its Solicitor's bill of costs, amounting to £191 10s., and voting gratuities to the Clerk and Beadle. A Committee was also appointed to wait upon Sir William Young (Secretary for War), and Lord Duplin, to convey to them the thanks of the Company for their extraordinary services in Parliament.

Encouraged by its previous successes, and fortified by the knowledge that it had such powerful friends in the House of Commons as the two gentlemen above named, the Court lost no time in proceeding with that portion of the Company's parliamentary requirements which related to the importation of Gold and Silver Lace, etc.; and which had not been dealt with in the Act recently obtained.   Accordingly, in March, 1 74⅔, such effective steps had been taken, that leave was given to Lord Duplin, Sir W. Young, and Mr. Alderman Heathcote (the late Lord Mayor), to prepare and bring in a Bill intituled, " For the more effectually " preventing the Importation and Wear of Gold and Silver Lace, " Thread, Fringe, etc., or other work made of Gold and Silver Wyre, " manufactured abroad."

H. C. J. xxiv. p. 445.

Ibid., p. 466.

This Bill was duly brought in by Lord Duplin, and passed the House of Commons ; and the Secretary for War was instructed to take it to the House of Lords ; an additional clause having been inserted, " allowing a person entering the Country to import two new suits for his " or her own wear."

H. L. J. xxvi. 16 Geo. II. pp. 235, 238, and 243. Ibid., pp. 248, 250, and 253.

The Bill was read a first and second time in the House of Lords, and committed.   Its consideration in Committee was, however, several times postponed, until at last the vacation ensued, and the Bill fell through.

H. C. J. xxv. 22 Geo. II. pp. 800 and 811.

After meeting with this check, the Company thought it advisable to let the matter rest for a while ; but six years later, viz. in March, 1748, it returned to the charge ; for the Parliamentary Records show that the Bill was again introduced by Lord Duplin ; it passed rapidly through the House, and Sir W. Young was ordered to take it up to the Lords.

Ibid., pp. 844, 850, and 859.

H. L. J. xxvii. 22 Geo. II. pp. 340, 341, 343, 350.

A fortnight sufficed to see the Bill passed through the Upper Chamber, and the Royal Assent was given on May 26, 1749.

This Act, which was a very short one, re-enacted the same penalties, viz. Seizure and Public burning of the goods, plus a Fine of One Hundred Pounds to be paid by the person so importing or selling Foreign-made Embroidery, Gold or Silver Thread, and Lace, Fringe, Brocade, or Gold or Silver Wire and Plate.   The wearer, however, was to incur no penalty.

Such are the Acts obtained by the Gold and Silver Wyre-Drawers Company : and it may be safely asserted that they form a very creditable record of Parliamentary work, successfully carried through for the advancement and benefit of the Trade.

These Acts, Five in number, have all been subsequently repealed.

The following notes, taken from the Minute Books of the proceedings of the Court of Assistants, during the period of time dealt with in this Chapter, are of interest, as illustrating the action taken by the Company in reference to the various Acts of Parliament just described.

April 10th, 1701. The Master reported that, together with the Wardens and others, he had made search for, and had found a quantity of defective and ill-wrought wares, which were duly cut. One of the Wardens also reported that resistance was made to the search by two persons. The Court thereupon resolved to prosecute the offenders at law.

May 27, 1701. The Court ordered a number of persons to be prosecuted for denying search, etc.

Oct. 22, 1701. The Court decided to consult Mr. Northy, the Attorney-General, as to whether the By Laws were strong enough to enable it to prosecute Members of the Company for transgressing certain of the Ordinances. Mr. Northy's opinion was given in favour of the Company.

Dec. 3, 1701. Mr. Washburne, on making submission (already referred to), prayed that when members of the Court came to his house to make search, none of them who used any Engines might go into his working-room. This was granted; and shows that, even in these early days, regard was had for the secrets and mysteries of the Art.

Dec. 8, 1720. Petition presented to the Master and Wardens against the employment by Free-Masters, of Foreigners, and non-freemen, in the Trade.

1730. Resolution passed by the Court that The Company will stand by and assist every person who shall seize and condemn any Foreign Gold and Silver Lace that shall hereafter be imported into the Kingdom, and will pay the costs of such proceedings if unsuccessful; but if a Verdict be obtained, then the costs shall come out of the penalty of One Hundred Pounds.

1731. Advertisements ordered to be inserted in the Newspapers *re* the importation of Foreign Lace.

1732. Mr. John Blachford (afterwards Sheriff), and Mr. Samuel Smith pleaded that, being free of the Goldsmiths Company, they were not liable to serve any Offices in the Gold and Silver Wyre-Drawers Company; and they were accordingly discharged from the Office of Wardens.

1732. Law suit which had been pending for two or three years against Mr. Peter Hammond, for refusing to take up the Office of Assistant, was concluded. His Attorney paying costs and fees to the Company.

1733. Further seizure of Foreign Lace reported to the Court.

1735. Advertisements *re* importation of Foreign Lace repeated in the Newspapers and a reward of Five Pounds offered for information.

1735. Foreign Lace seized was condemned in the Court of Exchequer.

1735. Resolution passed, no longer to pay the reward of five per cent. on Foreign Lace imported and seized, unless the same be burnt or destroyed.

1748. Information was given to the Court that large quantities of French Lace and Embroidery were being brought into the Country; whereupon it was unanimously resolved to indemnify the Master and Wardens, and likewise Informers, against any expense that might arise in consequence of their seizing the same.

1764. His Majesty's Customs informed the Company that they wanted a person to attend at the Custom House, Three times a week, to inspect Foreign Lace. It was resolved that the Master and Wardens do confer with the Weavers' Company; and in the meantime that Mr. Low (afterwards succeeded by Mr. Dell, a Member of the Court) be appointed at a Salary of eight shillings per week.

1761. (From the Account-Book.) Gratuity of Nine Guineas paid to sundry persons for seizing " Blown Lace."

1764. Details of expenses incurred at the Burning of Lace.

1765. Abraham Prado paid One Hundred Pounds penalty for importing Foreign Lace. The account book of same date records that the Company paid to the King Fifty pounds out of this penalty. Also that much time was spent at the Custom House, and large payments made for legal and other expenses in connection with these proceedings.

1766. Three hundred pounds penalty recovered from Mr. John Schütz, on account of Trial that had been pending for some time past, for Importation of Foreign Lace.

1764. A Mr. Pont was summoned to "ye Court of Conscience" for non-payment of Quarterage.

1772. Ex'es at the Half Moon Tavern at a Burning—

Clothes	...	...	2	14	0
Lace	...	...	1	9	3
Sundries	...	...	1	2	0
			5	5	3

1773. A Resolution was carried that for the future the Stewards should pay a Fine of Ten Pounds, and that the Company would provide the Annual Feast.

1780. Stewards Fine reduced to Five Pounds for all who were on the Livery; and resolution passed to return the sum of £5 to those who had already served as Steward, if they took up the Livery.

Several matters of interest relating to the general history of the Company, are also mentioned in the Minute books of this period, viz. :—

Dec. 17, 1719. The Committee delivered a copy of the Title of the Charter of Incorporation to Mr. Pears Maudnitt, of the Herald's Office ; in order to have it inserted in Stow's Survey of London, which was then about to be reprinted ; but, although an Appendix was added to this work in 1720, the information afforded by the Company does not appear to have been included therein.

Mar. 10, 1720. The Court resolved to endeavour to obtain a grant from the Court of Aldermen, constituting the Company one of the Livery Companies of the City of London. No further mention is however made of the matter for many years.

1738. The Freedom of the Company was presented to George Stead, Thomas Woodward, Joseph Heywood, Samuel Spingle, and to Messrs. Plummer and Vaughan.

1741.   The Court resolved to purchase a Common Seal for the use of the Company, but one of the Wardens, Mr. Nicholas Cunliffe, who became Master in 1743, had the Arms of the Company very handsomely engraved upon a Silver Seal, which he then presented to the Court, and which is still used by the Company.

1755.   Mr. John Waller, Wyre-Drawer, and Warden of the Company, who became Master in 1758, published a pamphlet entitled, " An Appeal to the Nobility and Gentry," and dealing with the question of the quality of English-made Gold and Silver Lace, Brocade, etc.

In this pamphlet he drew attention to the superiority of the foreign work over the English, and claimed to have proved his statements and figures before the Royal Society. Mention was made that a M. Chatalan, Laceman at Amsterdam, had laid out Three Thousand Pounds in Mills for flatting Gold and Silver Wire; and that the forged mills made at Leipsic were the best that they (? English or Flemish makers) had ever had.

Mr. Waller also claimed to have completed the Art of refining Steel.

He recited the Oath of Warden of the Gold and Silver Wyre-Drawers Company, which " he had sworn four times."

The Commissioners of the Treasury, in reporting on this matter, recommended that " There should be an Assay Master appointed for the making of Gold and Silver Wyre, as then was for Gold and Silver Plate at Goldsmiths Hall.

A copy of this interesting little publication is preserved in the library of the British Museum.

The following curious episode in the History of the Company will fitly conclude the present Chapter.

In the Year 1761, the Members of the Gold and Silver Wyre-Drawing Trade, who then composed this Worshipful Company, found themselves, like Frankenstein, confronted with a monster of their own creation; for, having in less prosperous times framed the By Law limiting to two the number of Apprentices to be taken or kept by any member of the Company at any one time, with a view to avoid the inconveniences then suffered by other trades (in consequence of the Members thereof being permitted to take an unlimited number of Apprentices), and also in order to ensure that " The youths put out to " the said Trade as Apprentices might, after they had served a laborious " Apprenticeship, be able to live and support themselves and families " as Journeymen in a comfortable manner, as persons in such a situation " of life might reasonably thinking expect or deserve."

When, (to again quote the wording of the period,) " The Masters of " the said Company had become more numerous, and the use of or call " in the said trade by the nobility and gentry had become much more " great," it was found that the then number of hands or journeymen were insufficient to do the amount of work required of them, and this evil was aggravated by the conduct of the men, who, (to once more quote the quaint phraseology used to describe their behaviour,) " Instead " of making a just and proper use of the care and indulgence of the " said Company towards them by preserving the trade in a good and " proper medium for their living and support had taken a quite contrary " course, and by degrees, from the time of making the said orders, " rules, and ordinances, down to the present time, had risen to such an " Intollerable, Insufferable, and Insupportable height of self sufficiency, " disobedience, and misbehaviour towards the Masters, Members of the " said Company, not in the least submitting to their Government, " Management, and Direction," which was regarded as a most Grievous and Insupportable Imposition both on the Masters and Customers, " and most unreasonably and without any just cause, exorbitantly and " insufferably exacting and demanding of the Masters, Members of the " said Company, most unreasonable wages, losing the time of their said " Masters by frequent and almost continued rioting, drunkenness, " debauchery, combinations, and confederacies together, not only to the " hurt and prejudice of themselves and their own families, but likewise " to the great oppression, hurt, and damage of their Masters who pay " them, so that it was Impossible for the said Masters to get a reason- " able Support by their business unless they in like manner raised their " prices upon their Customers, to the certain very great and unreason- " able abuse of the Nobility and Gentry of the Nation, and others " employing them, and undeignably and contradictory to, and evidently

"against the true intent and meaning of the said Letters Patent or
" Charter."

The Masters, therefore, most of whom were members of the
Company, brought their complaints under the notice of the Court.

The Master, Wardens, and Assistants of the Company, having
made due inquiry into this matter, and conceiving it to be their duty
" to take all reasonable and lawful measures to remedy these grievances,
"and to prevent the subjects being imposed upon," came to the conclusion that, " There was no readier, more perfect or legal method or
" way to check, control, or dissipate such unwarrantable, unjust and
"illegal practices of the Journeymen," than by making a new By Law
for the enlarging of the number of Apprentices, and thus bring the
pressure of competition to bear upon these unruly members of the
Trade.

Accordingly, it was unanimously resolved, that " for the future, it
"should be lawful for the Master, Wardens, and Court of Assistants of
" the Company of Gold and Silver Wyre-Drawers, each, and every one
"of them, to take and keep three Apprentices at one time, and no
" more."

The Lord Mayor & the Livery Companies on their way to Westminster in 1750

CHAPTER XI.

HE Gold and Silver Wyre-Drawers Company may be said, about this time, to have reached its Zenith; and all unconscious of the decay and paralysis that were impending over it and the Trade it represented, caused by the complete change in Fashion and in men's ideas brought about by the French Revolution, the Court resolved, in 1771, to renew the application unsuccessfully made in 1720, to the Lord Mayor and Court of Aldermen, praying that a Livery might be granted to the Company.

No steps, however, appear to have been taken in the matter until January 13, 1780, when the Court "Ordered that the resolution of the "10th of January, 1771 (for the Lord Mayor and Court of Aldermen to "be petitioned to grant a Livery to this Company) be forthwith carried "into execution."

It also resolved to start a subscription for this purpose; and further decided, "That any money subscribed by any member be considered "as part of his Livery Fine if the Company's petition should be

"granted ; but in case the same should be denied, the money was to
"go towards the cost of the petition, and the overplus to be returned
"to the subscribers."

And it appears from the Accounts for this year that the sum
of £68 5s. was accordingly collected from the members of the
Company.

Success on this occasion attended the efforts of the Gold and Silver
Wyre-Drawers; for the Committee appointed by the Court of Aldermen on June 6, 1780, to consider the petition of the Company, reported
in its favour as follows : "That divers Members of the said Company
"were of considerable Substance, and able and willing to bear the
"expense attending on a Livery, and to contribute and assist on all
"public occasions to the Honour, Dignity, and Service of the City.
"That the Petitioners humbly apprehended that if a Livery were
"granted to the said Company it would be of great benefit and advan-
"tage thereto, and an Encouragement to a valuable and extensive
"branch of the British Trade. That persons using the Art and
"Mystery of Drawing and Flatting of Gold and Silver Wyre, etc, etc,
"would be more ready to take up the freedom of the Company; and
"Merchants, Warehousemen, and other Traders and Exporters of
"Gold and Silver Lace, although not makers thereof, would become
"Members of the said Company. And that they (the Committee)
"were therefore of opinion that the Company should be created and
"made a Livery Company of this City." The Court of Aldermen, on
July 18, 1780, accordingly approved and confirmed the report, which
was ordered to be entered in the Repertory, the Livery Fine being
fixed at the sum of Fifteen pounds to the Company, Five Shillings to
the Clerk, and two Shillings and sixpence to the Beadle.

The expenses attending this Livery Grant amounted to £47 12s. 6d.
in addition to sundry Gratuities given to certain Clerks who had
interested themselves in the matter.

Many members of the Company at once took up the Livery ; and
the accounts for that year show that the Fines paid in connection
therewith amounted to nearly Three hundred pounds ; a very welcome
addition to the Company's Funds, and which served to re-establish its
finances on a more satisfactory footing.

One of the first investments subsequently made, was the purchase of a Beadle's Staff with a very handsome Silver head, bearing the Arms of the Company, and costing the sum of Seventeen pounds ten shillings.

CHAPTER XII.

AVING dealt in the foregoing pages with the rise and progress of the Gold and Silver Wyre-Drawers Company, and of the Trade with which it had been inseparably connected, it is now the painful duty of the historian to chronicle the decay and fall of that once-flourishing industry, and consequently of the Incorporated Society which had done so much for its advancement and welfare.

Partly owing to the caprices of that fickle Goddess " Fashion," who for nearly three hundred years had so greatly befriended the Wyre-Drawers, and partly, as before stated, in consequence of the change which came over men's ideas about the period of the Great French Revolution, Gold and Silver Lace was no longer in demand ; and the inevitable result ensued, viz. that the Trade began to wither and decay.

Happily, however, one can pass lightly over this painful epoch in the chequered career of the Gold and Silver Wyre-Drawers Company ; mainly owing to the fact that but little that is worthy of note occurred during this period of the Company's existence, and also because brighter times were coming, upon which it is both permissible and pleasurable to dwell.

It is, however, of interest to observe that in spite of the bad times that were impending, the Court of the Company relaxed none of its vigilance. Thus, in 1789, when a certain Mr. Pitcher, a member of the Company, "in consequence of a combination amongst the Journeymen" applied to the Court of Aldermen for leave to license three foreigners to work at the Trade, the Court at once determined to resolutely oppose the application.

This opposition was carried through successfully; the Court of Aldermen refusing the application, and at the same time advising the Court of Assistants to adjust and settle the prices to be paid by the Masters in the Trade to their Journeymen; which was accordingly done; and a copy of the prices then fixed is given in the Appendix.

Mr. Pitcher, however, proved very obstinate; and being resolved to petition the Right Worshipful the President, Treasurer, Auditor-General, and the rest of the Governors of Bridewell and Beth'lem Hospital to be admitted one of the Art Masters of Beth'lem Hospital, the Court determined to inform the said Governors of the Rules laid down in the Charter and By-Laws of the Company; and also that in consequence of the declining state of the Trade, it had recently rescinded the New By-Law, made in 1761, enlarging the number of Apprentices that might be employed; and furthermore that the present state of the Trade precluded the possibility of any increase in the number of hands.

Mr. Pitcher was also summoned before the Court to show cause why he should not pay the penalty he had incurred for employing persons not free of the Company, and this gentleman still proving recalcitrant, the inevitable lawsuit ensued, which was eventually settled to the satisfaction of the Company, by the submission of the Offender, and the payment of the Fine.

The Minute-book shows that, as late as 1826, the Court was taking action against certain persons for offences contravening the By-Laws, and, even in 1873, it instructed the Clerk to institute legal proceedings against a member of the Company, for non-payment of his admission Fees, and the amount was duly recovered.

Strenuous efforts also appear to have been made from time to time to better the financial position of the Company. One of the two annual Feasts, viz. that celebrated on Lord Mayor's Day, was discontinued "For reasons of economy," and several of the Committee meetings were also dispensed with for the same motive.

Committees of ways and means were likewise appointed, which reported in favour of an increase in the Livery, the curtailment of the privilege of inviting friends to the Company's dinners, and of a reduction in the Fees payable on admission.

In 1802 the Court resolved to migrate from the Half Moon Tavern in Cheapside (where it had met for the last Sixty Years) to the George and Vulture Tavern in Cheapside; and it subsequently decided that its meetings should be held at the Clerk's Office, and its dinners be given at the Albion Tavern.

Frequent commutations of Quarterage, by the usual payment of twenty-one shillings, took place during this period.

The Court, in 1826, prepared a petition to the House of Commons, praying that the Excise Duties upon the Manufactures of this Company might be repealed; and it was forwarded to Mr. Huskisson for presentation.

In the following year the Court presented the Freedom of the Company to Mr. Samuel Lepard (the Clerk), who had done so much to maintain the interests of the Company for several years past, and who, eventually, ably served the office of Clerk for Forty-one years; this, with one exception, viz. that of his predecessor William Robins, who acted during Forty-two years, being the longest period of service recorded in the annals of the Company.

The Company, in 1834, gave full particulars to the Commissioners appointed to inquire into the Municipal Corporations, and the answers then given are duly recorded in the Minute-Book of that year's proceedings.

In 1837, the Company is seen to have joined the other City Companies who assisted at the reception of the Queen at St. Paul's Cathedral.

In 1849, Mr. James Scovell, Past Master, who had been a member of the Court of Assistants for Forty-four years, presented the Company

with a very handsome silver Loving-Cup, on the occasion of his retire-
ment from the Court. This gift was duly acknowledged ; and the vote
of thanks recording the same was engrossed on vellum and presented
to Mr. Scovell at a Banquet held at the Star and Garter Hotel,
Richmond.

But by far the most important action taken by the Company during
this period, and one testifying to the liberal views held at that time by
it members, consisted in the extension, in 1831, of the Freedom of the
Company to members of the Jewish faith.

This line of conduct reflects the greater credit upon the Gold and
Silver Wyre-Drawers' Company, inasmuch as at that time, the Jews did
not enjoy Municipal Rights in the City of London ; and to this Company therefore belongs the honour of having created, in 1831, in the
person of Mr Michael Solomon, the first Hebrew Freeman of the
City.

In consequence of this action, and of an eloquent letter written by
Mr. Solomon to his friends and acquaintances, which letter is recorded
on the Minutes of the Court, many Jews shortly afterwards joined the
Company.

In 1856, a letter of congratulation was sent to Sir David Salomon,
Lord Mayor, " recording the satisfaction of the Court at witnessing, in
"the Election of his Lordship, the progressive development of those
"liberal views which led this Court to admit Mr. Michael Solomon to
"the Freedom of the Company, and who became in consequence the
"first Hebrew Freeman of the City of London."

And in 1859, the House of Commons having passed a Resolution
by which members of the Hebrew Nation were admitted to take their
seats in that House, the Court "thought the time had arrived when it
"might with propriety (having been the first to extend the privilege
"of Citizenship to the Hebrews), bring the expression of its views
"under the notice of Baron Lionel de Rothschild, and congratulate
"him upon being the first Hebrew to take his seat in the House of
"Commons."

Nothing more of interest, during this period, remains to be
chronicled ; indeed the Company, in the last few years of the second
century of its existence, appears to have fallen into a semi-moribund

condition, from which it was only rescued, in 1879, by the energetic efforts of the newly appointed Clerk, Mr. Wynne E. Baxter, Under-Sheriff of the City of London, who introduced many gentlemen of position and influence to the Company; and the result of whose exertions is shown in the following and concluding chapter of this History.

PHŒNIX

CHAPTER XIII.

THE history of the Gold and Silver Wyre-Drawers
Company during the last twelve years, viz. from
1879 down to the present time, is marked by ever-
increasing prosperity; the experience and intimate
knowledge of Civic matters possessed by the Clerk,
aided by the persevering efforts of the recently
augmented Court of Assistants, where the energy
of the newer members was tempered by the wisdom of the seniors,
soon sufficed to once more launch the good old Ship on the flowing
tide of success.

A steady influx of high-class men set in, notably amongst them,
Colonel Sewell; George Kenning; Major Joseph, C.C.; Gabriel Lindo;
Major (afterwards Colonel) Duncan, M.P. for Finsbury, whose untimely
death the Company, in common with the whole Country, has recently
had to deplore; Major George Lambert, Past Prime Warden of the
Goldsmith's Company; and many others, each and all of whom exerted
themselves to the utmost to introduce fresh members on to the
Company.

Later on, many of the higher officers of the Corporation of the

City of London, of whom no less than Ten Members of the Court of Aldermen, Sir William Charley (Common Sergeant), Mr. Deputy Ashby, and others, took up the Freedom and Livery of the Gold and Silver Wyre-Drawers' Company.

Such representative men as Augustus Harris and Colonel North also became members of this ancient Guild.

The dignity and importance of the Company were greatly enhanced by the addition of such men to its Members ; and during the last six years, it has had the honour of including on its roll the names of two Lord Mayors, viz. Sir Polydore de Keyser and Sir Henry Aaron Isaacs, and four times during this period have both the Sheriffs of London and Middlesex been members of the Gold and Silver Wyre-Drawers Company, viz.—

In 1885, Alderman and Sheriff Evans ; Mr. Sheriff Clarke.

In 1887, Major (afterwards Alderman) and Sheriff Davies ; Mr. Sheriff Higgs.

In 1889, Alderman and Sheriff Gray ; Mr. Sheriff (afterwards Alderman) Newton.

In 1890, Alderman and Sheriff Stuart Knill ; Mr. Sheriff Walter Harris.

In 1890–91, Mr. Sheriff Augustus Harris.

This increase in the importance of the Company naturally carried with it certain public functions. Thus, in 1885, the Gold and Silver Wyre-Drawers are seen taking part, first in the Sheriffs' procession to Guildhall, and later on in the Lord Mayor's procession of that year.

As this was the first time that the Company had taken part in this annual Pageant, a great effort was made to signalize the event in a fit and worthy manner, and, thanks to the exertions of the Master, Major Joseph, and to the skill, taste, and generosity of Past-Master George Kenning, who, at his own expense, fitted up on Trolleys, a most picturesque and realistic representation of the Art of Gold and Silver Wyre-Drawing, as practised at the time when the Company was Incorporated, a display was made which was generally pronounced to be the chief feature of the Show.

The thanks of the Lord Mayor and Sheriffs' Committees

were voted to the Company for the part it had taken in the Procession.

In the following year the Court entertained the retiring Sheriffs at a complimentary Banquet given at the Albion Tavern, and presented them with illuminated addresses on vellum, recording its deep appreciation of the manner in which they had discharged the duties of their high office.

The Gold and Silver Wyre-Drawers are again seen, in 1887, to be numbered amongst the Livery Companies who accompanied the Lord Mayor to the Royal Courts of Justice, this being the first time in the history of the Company that it had had the honour to include amongst its members the Chief Magistrate and Head of the City of London.

It may not be out of place to mention here, that the Court showed its appreciation of this distinction which had fallen upon the Company, by subscribing for and presenting to Sir Polydore and Lady De Keyser, a very handsome silk Screen, embroidered with the Arms of the City of London, in Gold and Silver Wire in "proper colours," and with a suitable inscription, expressing the gratification of the Company at the high honour attained to by one of its Members.

In 1888, the Gold and Silver Wyre-Drawers, for the second time, took part in the Sheriffs' procession from the Clothworkers' Hall to Guildhall ; and in the following year, when the Lord Mayor and both the Sheriffs were again members of the Company, they once more joined the annual civic Pageant.

On this occasion also, a successful attempt was made to represent the Trade of the Company ; special liveries, trimmed with Gold and Silver Lace, and cut after the fashion of the time of Elizabeth, were made for the coachmen and footmen, and representatives of the supporters to the Arms, viz. a Throwster and an Indian, walked, attired in "proper costume," on either side of the Master's carriage.

The hearty congratulations and good wishes of the Court were also voted to Alderman Sir Henry A. Isaacs, on his election to the high and important office of Lord Mayor, and to Alderman Stuart Knill and Mr. Walter Harris on their election as Sheriffs ; and these resolutions were emblazoned on vellum, and presented at a complimentary Banquet given by the Master, Gabriel Lindo, Esq., at the Criterion Restaurant, to the Lord Mayor and Sheriffs, and to the Court of Assistants.

Notwithstanding the expenses attendant on these public functions, etc., it is gratifying to note that the Funds of the Company remain in a satisfactory condition.

At the commencement of the period of which this Chapter treats, the amount invested was £700; it is now £1300; the difference between these amounts, added to the sum of £410, expended in 1883, in the purchase of Freehold Ground Rents at Barnsbury Square, Islington, makes up a total of £1010, which has been saved and invested during the past twelve years.

The other worldly possessions of the Company have likewise increased; the retiring Masters, and the Members of the Court who had attained to the Shrievalty, having presented the Company with Banners of their Arms, and other handsome gifts.

In 1880, the members of the Court each subscribed Two Guineas for the purchase of the very handsome gold and enamelled Badge, representing the Arms of the Company, which is worn by the Master upon all State occasions.

In this year the Lord Mayor and Sheriffs, for the first time, honoured the Company with their presence at the Annual Banquet, which graceful compliment had been annually repeated ever since.

In 1881, the Company gave full information to the Commissioners for Inquiry into the Livery Companies of the City of London, and a full report of the answers furnished is printed in the Blue Book issued by the Commissioners.

In 1884, the thanks of the Company were voted to Past-Master George Kenning, for the interesting Exhibition of Gold and Silver Wyre-Drawing, made at his own expense (but with which the name of the Company was connected), in "Old London Street" at the International Health Exhibition.

Another critical stage of the Company's existence was reached in 1888, when it was found that, in consequence of the efforts that had been made during recent years, and of the growing popularity and reputation of the Gold and Silver Wyre-Drawers' Company, the limit of One hundred, prescribed by the Livery Grant of 1780, had been reached, and therefore, although several gentlemen of position and influence were anxious to join the Company, it was impossible to make any addition to the number of its members.

The Court accordingly resolved to petition the Court of Aldermen "to increase the Livery of the Company to Two hundred, or such "other number as their honourable Court might think fit."

The Master and Wardens were then summoned before the Court of Aldermen to explain the object of this application, and to show cause why it should be granted ; and this having been done, That honourable Court was pleased to accede to the Company's request, and accordingly increased the limit of the Livery from One hundred to One hundred and fifty, and, at the same time, raised the Fine for admission thereto to Twenty-five Guineas.

All anxiety as to the future having been removed by this gracious and timely act of the Court of Aldermen, the Company was enabled to pursue the even tenour of its way, and in 1890, being mindful of the desire expressed by the Master in the name of the Company, on the occasion of the application for increasing the Livery, the Court resolved to make some effort to further the cause of Technical Education with respect to the Trade which the Company represents.

It accordingly decided to accept the offer of the Secretary to the Royal Military Exhibition, about to be held at Chelsea, to allot a space to the Company for the purpose of making a display of specimens of work in Gold and Silver Wire and Lace in all the various branches and stages of manufacture.

This decision was duly carried out, and a very interesting collection of work connected with the Gold and Silver Wyre-Drawers' Company, and its Trade, was shown at this Exhibition.

The following report was made by the Committee appointed to carry out the arrangements for this Exhibition : "Your committee in "the first place put themselves in communication with the various "members of the company, and, subsequently, with the valued assist- "ance of Past-Masters Kenning and Stewart, called personally upon "other gentlemen more immediately connected with the trade. After

"a careful examination of the specimens in the warehouses of these
"latter gentlemen, your committee selected a number of appropriate
"articles, which were generously lent for exhibition by (among others)
"Messrs. Kenning, Stanton, Benton and Johnson, Simpson and Rook,
"and J. B. Corney, to all of whom the committee are much indebted
"for their kind and gratuitous assistance. The exhibits, in addition to
"those selected, comprised various articles being the property of the
"company, and they were tastefully arranged in a handsome show-case.
"The case was placed in a prominent position in the northern transept
"of the Exhibition. It was inspected and much admired by a large
"number of visitors, as was testified not only by personal observation,
"but by the receipt of many letters congratulating the company on the
"successful result of its new departure. It having been thought that
"some suitable memento of the exhibit should be presented to the
"members of the company and others, your committee, after carefully
"considering the matter, decided that a souvenir card should be
"engraved, and this was done, and a copy sent to every member of
"the company, and also to those gentlemen who had contributed to the
"exhibit, as well as to the Lord Mayor and to the masters of the
"several livery companies. The Committee likewise sent tickets of
"admission to all the foregoing, with a notification drawing their special
"attention to the exhibit of the Gold and Silver Wyre-Drawers'
"Company." After alluding to the expenditure the exhibit entailed
upon the Company, the committee, in conclusion, thank the various
gentlemen who were instrumental in promoting the success of the
exhibit. "The most prominent among these are Past-Master Stewart
"and also Past-Master Kenning, who devoted much valuable time
"and attention to the arrangements at the Exhibition, and Miss Ethel
"Wright, who skilfully designed the memento card referred to above,
"and whose artistic help has been throughout of much service to the
"committee."

The Court also resolved that a sum of £105 should be set
aside for the purpose of apprenticing boys and girls to the business
of Gold and Silver Wyre-Drawing, or any trade in connection
therewith.

And in consequence of the heavy expenses attending the carrying out of the above Resolutions, the Court decided to forego, for this year, the annual Banquet to the Livery.

Reference having been made in former passages to the shrinking and decaying, at a previous period of the Company's history, of the Gold and Silver Wyre-Drawers' Trade, consequent upon a change in fashion having set in, it is but right to state that, although fewer persons are undoubtedly now employed than was the case in former years, probably owing to the concentration of this business into a lesser number of hands, and also to the extensive introduction of costly and intricate machinery, it is nevertheless a fact that the Trade, as at present constituted, is in a very satisfactory and flourishing condition; the Factories appear to be admirably managed, and the work-people happy and contented. And although, as in the past, there still are secrets connected with "the Trade, Art, and Mystery of Drawing and Flatting "of Gold and Silver Wyre, and the Makeing and Spinning of Gold and "Silver Thread and Stuffe," the Manufacturers are most courteous in showing members of the Company over their works, a visit to which will be found both interesting and instructive.

The following extract, from an article published in 1889 in the March number of *Chambers's Journal*, may be of interest to those who are not intimately acquainted with the process by which silver bars are transformed into gold thread.

" In the first place the silver is brought from the Bank of England "in cakes, weighing about one thousand ounces. To secure the "necessary degree of tenacity, a certain proportion of copper is added, "and the alloyed metal, in the form of cylindrical bars, is next "thoroughly heated.

" The hammering process follows; and the bars—originally about " two feet in length and two inches in diameter, but now half as long "again, and proportionately thinner—are in the next place filed and "rubbed until their surfaces are perfectly even.

" What we may call the second part of the process begins with the "laying on of leaf after leaf of gold in the proportion of two per cent. "Afterwards, each bar is wrapped in paper and well heated in a "charcoal fire. A sort of vice stands ready ; and in it bar after bar, "as it comes from the fire, is fixed and thoroughly burnished. All

"trace of its silver original has now disappeared, and the bar is ready
"for conversion into wire. This is accomplished by drawing it from
"one hundred to one hundred and fifty times through ever-diminishing
"holes in steel plates ; and finally, when the capabilities of this metal
"have been exhausted, through apertures in diamonds, rubies, or
"sapphires.

"The delicate wire thus obtained must now be passed through the
"steel rollers of one of Herr Krupp's little ' flatting-mills.'

"This brings us to the final process—the spinning of the flattened
"wire round silk, to form the golden thread of commerce. These
"spinning-machines are worked (when it is available) by water,
"although steam-engines are sometimes used ; but water-power is
"considered to be more regular and even in its action.

"The bulk of the manufactured article finds its way, in the shape
"of silky gold thread, to India and the far East generally, where it is
"converted by skilled native labour into those gorgeous cloths and
"tissues in which the heart of the Oriental delights.

"Have we not here a striking illustration of the superiority of
"Western thought and enterprise over that of the soft and luxurious
"East ? By the aid of machinery and improved methods of working,
"we are enabled to compete with our Hindu fellow-subjects in one of
"their specialities despite the difficulties of transit, to say nothing of
"the expense of transporting goods so great a distance. However
"surprising the fact, we cease to wonder at it, after being assured that
"the Hindu with his manual process can only extract eight hundred
"yards of wire from a piece of silver the size of a florin, which would
"yield our manufacturers sixteen hundred yards.

"What a wonderful property does gold possess in its malleability !
"It is asserted that every ounce of the bars whose fortunes we have
"followed with no little interest, each containing only two per cent. of
"gold, will run to the length of from five hundred to two thousand five
"hundred yards ; and the amazing figure of five thousand yards is on
"record. This latter thread would be finer than human hair; but the
"extreme limit is not even yet reached.

"There is a tradition telling how an attempt was once made to
"produce a wire fine enough for use in a transit instrument. A solid

"gold wire was drawn by means of a copper cylinder to the length of "twenty thousand feet to the ounce ; but at that point the shadow of a "thread fell to pieces, and the astronomer was obliged to resort to his "usual spider's web."

Before leaving this, the latest portion of the Company's career, it seems but just to place on record the eminent services rendered by those who have had the management of the affairs of the Company during this period in their hands.

Where all have done so well it appears invidious to make a distinction, nevertheless a special word of recognition is due to the long-sustained and untiring exertions of the able Clerk of the Company, Wynne E. Baxter, Esq., J.P., D.L, whose honorary services, the Court, in 1884, showed its appreciation of by subscribing to and presenting him with a testimonial, consisting of his portrait painted by Mr. Cave Thomas.

To Past-Masters Kenning, and Major Joseph, C.C., a special tribute of gratitude is likewise due ; to the former, for his great assistance and liberal expenditure both of time and purse, in all matters connected with the public functions and exhibits of the Company, as well as in respect to those practical questions relating to the Trade, where his valuable experience as a Craftsman has ever been at the disposition of his colleagues ; and to the latter, for his never-flagging zeal in the cause of the Company, and for the immense influence exercised by him, not only during the three years when a grateful Court thrice elected him as Master, but both before and subsequently, by which he was enabled to introduce over fifty members to the Company whose interest he had so much at heart.

Lastly, mention must be made of the invaluable work that has been done by the present Master, Gabriel Lindo, Esq., during the two years in which he has so ably occupied the Chair, and in recognition of which the Court, in April, last elected him for the third time in succession to that high position.

Devoting his time, his influence, and his means unreservedly to the affairs of the Company, he has applied himself with the greatest single-mindedness to the furtherance of its best interests, and to the enhancement of its position amongst the Livery Companies of the City of London.

After successfully arranging the part which the Company took in the procession of 1889, the Master (as previously referred to), at his own expense, entertained the Lord Mayor and Sheriffs, and the members of the Court of Assistants, at a magnificent banquet, given at the Criterion Restaurant, on the occasion of the presentation of illuminated addresses of congratulation to Alderman Sir Henry A. Isaacs, and to Alderman Stuart Knill and Mr. Walter Harris, on their election to the offices of Lord Mayor and Sheriffs of London.

He then, in furtherance of the cause of Technical Education, organized and carried through the successful display made by the Company at the Royal Military Exhibition at Chelsea, and commemorated this event by having printed a very artistic souvenir card (designed by Miss Ethel Wright), which was presented to every member of the Company, the Lord Mayor, Sheriffs, and the Masters of all the Livery Companies of the City of London.

At the close of his second year of office the Master presented the Company with a very beautiful gold and enamelled Chain of Office, to be worn with the Master's Badge on all State occasions; and has inaugurated his third year in the Chair by arranging for a Ball to be given at the Whitehall Rooms of the Hotel Métropole, on the 16th of June of the present year.

During his two years of Office Mr. Lindo has been the means of introducing over twenty members on to the Livery of the Company, thus increasing its numbers to 141, and it may fairly be said that he has set these gentlemen a brilliant example of what a Master should be, when they, in their turn, may be called upon to fill this important position.

And now the historian's task is done; and it only remains to give expression, with the most full and entire confidence in its realization, to the hope that the Worshipful Company of Gold and Silver Wyre-Drawers, having, like the Phœnix of old, risen rejuvenated from its ashes, may enjoy an equally long career of renewed prosperity and usefulness ; and that its present and future members, wisely adapting themselves to the altered circumstances of the times, may find, not only within the limits of the Trade which the Company represents, but also in those larger questions affecting the general welfare, fresh scope for their energies, and a wider field in which to labour for the public good.

Finis.

APPENDIX.

LIST OF THE ACTS OF PARLIAMENT HAVING REFERENCE TO THE GOLD AND SILVER WYRE-DRAWERS.

1. 9 Will. III. cap. 39 (1698). Rep. Stat. Law Rev. Act, 1867 (*i.e.* 30 and 31 Vict. cap. 59).

2. 1 Anne cap. XI. Rep. Stat. Law Rev. Act, 1867.

3. 10 Anne, cap. 19. Rep. 33 & 34 Vict. c. 99.

4. 15 Geo. II. cap. 20 (1742). Rep. in part 6 Geo. IV. c. 105; Stat. Law Rev. Act 1867; 41 & 42 Vict. cap. 49, s. 86.

5. 22 Geo. II. cap. 36 (1749). Rep. 6 Geo. IV. cap. 105.

SUMMARY OF THE ACTS OF PARLIAMENT RELATING TO THE GOLD AND SILVER WYRE DRAWERS, FROM NOTES TAKEN FROM THE COLLECTION OF STATUTES AND ACTS IN THE LIBRARY OF THE BRITISH MUSEUM.

9 WILL. III. c. 39 (1698).

"An Act for settling and adjusting the proportion of Fine Silver (and) Silk Large Folio " for the better making of Silver & Gold Thread; and to prevent the Abuses of Edit. " (the) Wire-Drawers."

Sec. 1. Enacts that from the 24th day of July, 1698, all Silver Wire to be drawn for the making of Gold and Silver Thread shall hold at the least, 11 oz. 16 dwt. (of Fine Silver upon every pound weight) Troy: and that all Silver to be Gilt and made use in the Wire-Drawers' Trade shall be of the above quality, and not to have less than 4 dwt. of Fine Gold laid on to each pound weight of the same Silver: under a Penalty of Five Shillings per ounce for every ounce not so made.

Sec. 2. Regulates the proportions of Gold and Silver that shall be allowed to cover so many ounces of Silk, in the average proportion of about two parts of Silver to one of Silk.

Sec. 3. Prohibits the spinning of Copper, Brass, or other inferior metal upon Silk, and provides that it shall be spun upon Thread, Yarn, or Incle only.

I

Sec. 4. Prohibits the importation of Gold and Silver Thread, Lace, Fringe, or other work made thereof ; and also of Thread or Work made of Brass, Copper, or other inferior metal, into the kingdom of England, Dominion of Wales, or Town of Berwick upon Tweed, under pain of being forfeited and burnt.

Sec. 5. Provides how Penalties shall be divided and recovered.

Sec. 6. Makes provisions for any actions arising out of the enforcement of this Act, and provides for the recovery of Treble Costs.

Sec. 9. Limits the duration of this Act to Three Years.

1 ANNE c. XI.

Large Folio
Edit.
" An Act for continuing and amending the Act made in the Ninth Year of " His late Majesties Reign, intituled An Act for the settling of the proportion of "Fine Silver and Silk etc." (repeats the preamble of the former Act).

This Act practically renews the old one ; and also provides that a Penalty of One hundred pounds, in addition to the previous forfeiture and burning, shall be paid by the Importer.

Sec. 8. Provides that the Act shall continue in force for Seven Years.

10 ANNE c. 19 (c. 26 in common printed editions).

Large Folio
Edit.
" An Act for laying additional duties on Hydes and Skins etc, etc, and new " duties on . . . and on Gilt & Silver Wire etc."

Secs. 48 to 68.

Sec. 48. Provides that for Thirty-two Years from July 1, 1712, a duty of One shilling per Ounce on all Gilt Wire, and Ninepence per Ounce on all Silver Wire, shall be levied upon all such Wire imported into the Kingdom of Great Britain. And imposes a duty of eightpence per Ounce upon all Gilt Wire, and of Sixpence per ounce upon all Silver Wire made in Great Britain.

Very strict regulations were laid down, and heavy penalties provided for non-compliance with the Clauses of this Act, dealing with the entries and returns to be made by Wyre-Drawers.   ·

Sec. 68. Enacts that during the continuance of the said Duties upon Gold and Silver Wire granted by this Act, No Gold or Silver Thread, Lace, Fringe, or other work made thereof, shall be imported into Great Britain, upon pain of being forfeited, and upon the further penalty of One hundred Pounds Fine.

15 GEO. II. c. 20 (1742).

Octavo Edit.
" An Act to prevent the counterfeiting of Gold & Silver Lace ; and for the " settling and adjusting the proportions of Fine Silver and Silk ; and for the " better making of Gold & Silver Thread."

This Act also practically renews the preceding ones, but this time for an indefinite period.

The same penalties are provided, and in addition, to ensure the quality of the Metal, it is enacted. "That the Ingot of Silver, before the Gold is applied, "shall be weighed in the presence of the Officer of Excise; and likewise after "the Gilding process has been effected ; in order to prove that the due amount of "Fine Gold, viz. 4 dwt. 4 grs. per pound weight (Troy) of Silver, has been put on. "And a penalty of Twenty pounds is to be imposed upon any person refusing to "admit the Officer to his Workshop or Warehouse."

All material made from Copper, etc., and to be used in Theatrical performances, was especially excepted from the provisions of this Act.

This Act was made a Public one, and took effect from July 1st, 1742.

22 GEO. II. c. 36 (1749).

"An Act for the more effectual preventing the importation and wear of Gold ^{Octavo Edit.} "& Silver Thread, Lace and other work made of Gold & Silver Wire manu- "factured in foreign parts."

This Act re-enacts the same penalties, viz. seizure and public burning of the Goods, plus a Fine of One hundred Pounds to be paid by the person so importing or selling Foreign-made Embroidery, Gold or Silver Lace, and Thread, Fringe, Brocade, or Gold or Silver Wire and Plate.

Sec. 7. Provides that the wearer is to incur no penalty, and shall be allowed, on entering the Country, to import two new suits for his or her own wear.

The Act to take effect from the 1st day of July, 1749.

LIST OF THE PRICES FOR WORK, TO BE PAID BY THE MASTER GOLD AND SILVER WYRE DRAWERS TO THE JOURNEYMEN EMPLOYED IN THE TRADE, AS SETTLED BY THE COURT OF THE COMPANY, IN 1779.

GOLD.				SILVER.			
For Bright	20d.	1/0	per oz.	For	16d.	8d.	per oz.
„ Rich	20d.	11½d.	„ „	„ Bright	14d.	7d.	„ „
„ Ordinary	20d.	11d.	„ „	„ Fine	14d.	7d.	„ „
„ Fine	18d.	10½d.	„ „	„ Common	14d.	5½d.	„ „
„ Common	18d.	9d.	„ „	„ Bright	12d.	5½d.	„ „
	16d.	7d.	„ „	„ Common	12d.	4½d.	„ „
	14d.	6d.	„ „		10d.	3½d.	„ „
	12d.	4d.	„ „		8d.	3d.	„ „
	10d.	3d.	„ „		6d.	2½.d	„ „
					4d.	2d.	„ „

Allowance for waste ...   ... 1/   Allowance for waste ...   ... 3d.

GOLD AND SILVER WYRE-DRAWERS COMPANY.

LIST OF THE MASTERS.

Date.	Name.	Date.	Name.
1693.	Nathaniel Smith.	1726.	Walter Crew.
1694.	The Same.	1727.	The Same.
1695.	Thomas Wright.	1728.	Godwin Washbourne.
1696.	Thomas Bracee, Captn.	1729.	The Same.
1697.	Daniel Biddle.	1730.	Daniel Mallory
1698.	Robert Rhodes.	1731.	The Same.
1699.	The Same.	1732.	The Same.
1700.	Daniel Field.	1733.	Lionel Barnes (died), Samuel Morris (successor).
1701.	Christopher Blower.		
1702.	The Same.	1734.	Richard Drury.
1703.	Henry Southouse.	1735.	The Same.
1704.	Francis Greene.	1736.	John Haynes.
1705.	Thomas Price.	1737.	The Same.
1706.	John Shayler.	1738.	John Dodsworth.
1707.	Edward Page.	1739.	Edmund Tanner.
1708.	Richard Andrew.	1740.	Richard Cook.
1709.	John Lane.	1741.	Robert Berkeley.
1710.	Charles Hosier.	1742.	Robert Pitter.
1711.	The Same.	1743.	Nicholas Cunliffe.
1712.	John French.	1744.	Robert Glyde.
1713.	Walter Turner.	1745.	Thomas Gardiner.
1714.	The Same.	1746.	John Embry.
1715.	Joseph Tucker.	1747.	Benjamin Lane.
1716.	The Same.	1748.	The Same.
1717.	Richard Taylor.	1749.	William Jephcote.
1718.	George Prestland.	1750.	Robert Crew.
1719.	The Same.	1751.	Samuel Crouch.
1720.	William Southouse.	1752.	John Walklate.
1721.	The Same.	1753.	Andrew Aylesbury.
1722.	Pauncefort Green.	1754.	John Court.
1723.	The Same.	1755.	The Same.
1724.	William Harker.	1756.	Daniel How.
1725.	The Same.	1757.	William Read.

Date.	Name.	Date.	Name.
1758.	John Waller.	1801.	William Turner (Jun.).
1759.	Samuel Plumb.	1802.	Thomas Chapman.
1760.	George Vaughan.	1803.	William Reeves.
1761.	The Same.	1804.	Henry Turner.
1762.	Hewson Scott.	1805.	James Norton.
1763.	Edmund Tanner.	1806.	John Uffington.
1764.	John Macartney.	1807.	John Mills.
1765.	Joseph Atkinson.	1808.	The Same.
1766.	Stephen Crouch.	1809.	Richard Lowther (Jun.).
1767.	William Dracutt.	1810.	Joseph Fearne.
1768.	Benjamin Goffe.	1811.	Lewis Miles.
1769.	Henry Questead.	1812.	Joseph Turner.
1770.	George Naylor.	1813.	The Same.
1771.	Thomas Brown.	1814.	The Same.
1772.	Thomas Dewin.	1815.	Thomas Boys (Jun.).
1773.	Benjamin Dewin.	1816.	The Same.
1774.	William Stackhouse.	1817.	The Same.
1775.	Adam Bellinger.	1818.	The Same.
1776.	Richard Sturley.	1819.	Robert Reynolds.
1777.	Samuel Roberts.	1820.	William James.
1778.	John Studdard.	1821.	Joseph Johnson.
1779.	William Turner.	1822.	Fearne (Sen.).
1780.	John Read.	1823.	James Scovell.
1781.	Thomas Taunton.	1824.	Samuel McClary.
1782.	William Gomme.	1825.	Nicholas Boys.
1783.	Joseph Carter.	1826.	Joseph Fearne.
1784.	Joseph Allen.	1827.	William Lewis.
1785.	Charles Scott.	1828.	Bilcliffe Martin.
1786.	John Scarnell.	1829.	James Reynolds.
1787.	John Miles.	1830.	Thomas Burgin.
1788.	Charles Lockwood.	1831.	Ferdinand R. Camroux.
1789.	Thomas Boys.	1832.	James Scovell.
1790.	William K. Wigginton.	1833.	William Walker.
1791.	William Stackhouse.	1834.	John Atherley.
1792.	John Richardson.	1835.	Henry Johnson Appleford.
1793.	Richard Lowther.	1836.	Edward Stillwell.
1794.	Richard Birch.	1837.	James Boys.
1795.	Samuel Fearne.	1838.	James Botson McClary.
1796.	Edward Hale.	1839.	George Scovell.
1797.	Edward Utton.	1840.	Henry Wm. Johnson.
1798.	John Proudley.	1841.	William Bullmore.
1799.	John Chupcey.	1842.	Thomas Hackett.
1800.	Edward Mottrom.	1843.	Michael Solomon.

Date.	Name.	Date.	Name.
1844.	Ferdinand F. Camroux.	1868.	George O. Camroux.
1845.	Alfred A. McClary.	1869.	William Mashman.
1846.	Henry Bland.	1870.	Frederick Stanton.
1847.	John Lane.	1871.	David Henry Jacobs.
1848.	Samuel McClary.	1872.	Edward Burke.
1849.	William Burgin.	1873.	Henry William Johnson.
1850.	Thomas Burgin (Jun.).	1874.	George Foster.
1851.	John Burgin (Jun.).	1875.	J. G. Johnson.
1852.	Benjamin White.	1876.	Francis Pendered.
1853.	Owen Clutton.	1877.	The Same.
1854.	Frederick J. Campbell.	1878.	George Davenport.
1855.	The Same.	1879.	The Same.
1856.	Richard M. Miles.	1880.	John K. Luck.
1857.	Edward S. Stillwell.	1881.	Thomas Gerrard Fletcher.
1858.	The Same.	1882.	George Kenning.
1859.	James R. Reynolds.	1883.	The Same.
1860.	George Benton.	1884.	Hymen A. Joseph (Major), C C.
1861.	George Simons.	1885.	The Same.
1862.	William Clayton.	1886.	The Same.
1863.	Charles F. Corney.	1887.	James Knapton Abel.
1864.	Edwin Newell.	1888.	Horace Stewart.
1865.	Charles Gammon.	1889.	Gabriel Lindo, C.C., F.R.G.S.
1866.	The Same.	1890.	The Same.
1867.	John W. Marshall.	1891.	The Same.

LIST OF THE CLERKS.

Date.	Name.
1694.	John Borrett (the City Solicitor).
1702.	William Borrett (Nephew to the above).
1714.	William Hilditch.
1718.	Samuel Briggs.
1721.	Andrew Osborne.
1739.	Nathaniel Stable and Joseph Brian.
1740.	Jasper Bull.
1748.	Thomas Harris.
1774.	Mr. Ducker.
1778.	William Robins.
1820.	Richard S. Taylor.
1822.	Jacob Mould.
1824.	Samuel Lepard.

1861. Samuel Lepard and Charles Gammon (jointly).
1865. Charles Gammon.
1879)
to } Wynne E. Baxter, J.P., D.L.
1891)

LIST OF THE BEADLES.

Date.	Name.
1694.	Richard Brady.
1701.	George Meakings.
1723.	John Leech.
1736.	Richard Drury.
1743.	Robert Wrathall.
1767.	James Dennis.
1796.	William K. Wigginton.
1810.	Richard Pugh.
1826.	John Burgin.
1856.	George Burgin.
1866.	Abraham Hervey.
1880.	Lovell.

COMPLETE LIST OF THE MEMBERS OF THE COMPANY, IN JUNE, 1891.

MASTER.
‡‡ GABRIEL LINDO, C.C., F.R.G.S.

WARDENS.

David Evans, J.P. (Alderman).
William Hays.

Edmond Frank Brewster Fuller.
Daniel Wellby, F.R.G.S.

COURT OF ASSISTANTS.

‡Ferdinand Ferguson Camroux.
Christopher Rook.
‡Henry William Johnson.
‡George Oliver Camroux.
‡‡George Davenport.
‡David Henry Jacobs.
‡‡Francis Pendered.
‡Thomas Gerrard Fletcher.
‡John Kinton Luck.
George Benton.
Thomas Davies Sewell (Lieut.-Col.).
Henry William Henniker Rance (LL.D. Cantab).
‡James Knapton Abel-Knapton.
‡‡George Kenning.
James Bishop.
Henry John Dore, F.R.G.S.
‡Horace Frederick Stewart.
Henry David Davis.
Edwin William Streeter, F.R.G.S.,

M.A.I., Gold Medalist of the " Royal Order of Frederic."
Thomas Alexander Ridpath.
‡‡‡Hymen Aaron Joseph (Major), C.C.
James Robert Brown, F.R.G.S.
Robert Barnes, M.D. Lond. and F.C.P.
James Sidebottom.
Edward Eyre Ashby (Deputy), H.M.L.
Edward Fenner.
George Lambert, (Major), F.S.A.
Thomas Clarke (Sheriff, 1885–6).
Stuart Knill (Alderman), (Ex-Sheriff).
Phineas Cowan (Alderman; Lieut.-Col.).
John William Robins, M.A., J.P.
Horatio David Davies, J.P. (Alderman and Colonel).
Sir Polydore de Keyser (Alderman).
George Robert Tyler (Alderman).
Woolfe Haldenstein.
John Thomas North (Colonel).

Wynne Edwin Baxter, J.P., D.L. (Clerk).

Marked thus ‡ have served the office of Master.
     ,,   ‡‡   ,,   ,,   ,,   twice.
     ,,   ‡‡‡   ,,   ,,   ,,   three times.

LIVERYMEN.

(In Order of Seniority.)

Wyndham, Robert Henry Sharpe.
Lambert, Alfred James.
Whitwham, Francis George.
Ingham, Edward, F.R.G.S.
Collison, Frederick Henry.
Charley, Col. Sir Wm., Q.C., D.C.L.
  (Common Sergeant).
Isaacs, Sir Henry Aaron (Alderman).
Harris, Augustus Henry Glossop
  (Sheriff).
Carvick, Henry Bruce Mayer (Capt.).
Proffitt, John.
Cohen, Benjamin Louis, L.C.C.
Webb, Matthew Righton, J.P.
Bertram, John.
Hawkins, Alfred Templeton, C.C.,
  J.P., D.L.
Squire, Henry, C.C.
Hepburn, John Frankland, C.C.
Ridley, Joseph James.
Durlacher, Alexander.
Lea, John Edward.
Viney, Cecil Thomas.
Arbib, Enrico.
Henry, John Sollie.
Cox, Edwin.
Price, Samuel, C.C.
Probyn, Leslie.
Heilbut, Samuel.
Cordner, William James.
Hodge, Baldwin.
Gray, Edward James (Alderman).
Harris, Arthur.
Parkington, John Roper (Captain.)

Pryke, William Robert, C.C.
Palmer, William.
Raynsford, Charles Arthur.
Meissner, William Henry.
Woodruff, William Thomas.
Von Joel, Henry.
Palmer, Thomas George Adams.
Chubb, John Charles, C.C.
Watson, Alfred.
Lee, Edward, C.C.
Newton, Alfred James (Alderman).
Renals, Joseph (Alderman).
Stapley, Richard, C.C.
Harris, Walter Henry (Ex-Sheriff).
Russell, David.
Gade, Frederick Theodore.
Wild, James Anstey (Registrar, City of
  London Court).
Hollington, Alfred Jordan, C.C., L.C.C.
Haldenstein, Henry Hymen.
Myers, Lewis Michael, C.C.
Ballantyne, James.
Beste, Henry Augustus.
Denney, John Edwin.
I'Anson, Edward Blakeway, C.C.
Mocatta, Charles Abraham.
Williamson, William Henry, C.C.
Appleford, Stephen Herbert.
D'Avigdor, Elim Henry.
Woolf, Sidney, Q.C.
Stanton, Edwin Alfred.
Stanton, Horace Frank.
Foster, Harry Seymour.

LIVERYMEN WHO HAVE NOT PAID STEWARD'S FINE.

Dignam, Sylvester.
Thurston, George Henry.
Thurston, Charles Omega.
White, Benjamin.

Wordley, William.
Munk, Frederick William.
Joseph, Greville Edmund (Capt.).
Luck, John Richard Whitmore.

Stillwell, Edward William.
Lingard, Alfred.
Fox, Edwin, Jun.
Barnes, Robert Sydenham Fancourt,
     M.D. and F.R.C.P. London.
James, Warren Samuel.
Gordon, Alexander (Major).
Greenwood, Henry William, C.C.
Pugh, Edward.
Baker, Richard.
Millington, Charles Leschalles.
Martin, Charles.
Hubbard, David John.
Bodily, Henry James (Rev.).

Gayford, Chesterfield William.
Blair, Thomas.
Thomson, Edmund Wainwright.
Edwards, Patrick John.
Smyth, Stewart (Rev.).
Ponzini, Francis Leopold.
Henle, Louis Anthony.
Henry, William Franklin.
Benn, James Edward Hamilton.
Benoliel, Judah.
Lindo, Moses Albert Norsa.
Morris, Howard Carlile, C.C.
Lindo, Arthur.

LIVERYMEN ELECTED BUT NOT YET SWORN IN.

Houlder, Charles Spencer, C.C.
Horniman, Frederick John.
Castello, Percy Manuel.
Colls, J. Howard.
Joseph, Edward.

SUMMARY OF "THE GOULD WYER DRAWERS'"

CHARTER OF INCORPORATION, 21 JAMES I., 1623.

The King, in consequence of the scarcity of money and coin within the Land, Preamble. which was considered to have partly arisen from the unlawful consumption thereof in the making of Gold and Silver Thread—had by Proclamation dated the 11th day of June, 1622, prohibited and forbidden the manufacture of these wares ; but finding it was very difficult, if not impossible, to suppress this Industry, on account of so many persons being engaged therein who had no other means of livelihood, and being informed by the Petitioners that it was possible to take such measures for the resettling of the Trade as would obviate this waste of Coin and Bullion, Resolved " That on the condition which had been " voluntarily offered by the Petitioners, That an equal amount of Foreign gold " and silver Coin and Bullion was imported from abroad to countervail that used " in the said manufactures, and that a duty of sixpence per oz. was paid upon all " gold and silver Wyer used in the Said Manufactures, and of four-pence for the " seal of every mark or pound of Gold and Silver Thread made up—the Petition " should be granted and that the Petitioning Gold and Silver Wyer Drawers, viz. " Matthias Fowle and some seventy-six others, all of whom were specified by Number of " name—should be henceforth forever One Fellowship and one Body Corporate Wyer- " and Politic in deed and in name." Drawers.

By the title of "Governor, Assistants, and Commonalty of Gould Wyer- Title of the Drawers of the City of London." Company.

It was ordained that they should be able and capable in law to have, purchase, Ordinary civil hold, and enjoy, Manors, lands, tenements, franchises, etc., and to demise, grant, rights granted. let, assign, or dispose of the same as fully as any other Corporation or Body Politic.

A Common Seal was granted, with power to alter, deface, break, and make Common Seal. new the same at their will and pleasure.

There were to be henceforth and forever, One Governor and Twenty-two Constitution of Assistants. the Court.

Only those who were free of the Company, and their workmen, journeymen, Restrictions as servants, and apprentices were to be allowed to practise, use, or exercise within to those per- the Realm of England and Dominion of Wales, the trades, mysteries, and at this In- manufactures of making Gold and Silver Thread and other Wares appertaining dustry. to these industries.

Machinery.   Power was given to the aforesaid to set up Engines, Frames, Mills, etc., etc., and to trade in and sell all such before mentioned goods.

First Governor.   Matthias Fowle was to be the first Governor for the term of his natural life. Twenty-two Assistants were named and constituted for life, viz :—

First Assistants.

Anthony Hardinge.	John Ball.
Robert Jenner.	Adolphus Fowle.
William Symonds.	William Leadsham.
Thomas Lee.	John Wollaston.
George Binge.	Francis King.
Christopher Goodlake.	John Eaton.
Hugh Cressy.	Joseph Symmonds.
Simon Owen.	John Rundell.
Thomas Williams.	John Ling.
Hugh Underhill.	John Lee.
Anthony Peniston.	Thomas Jackson.

Duration of Governor's term of Office.
Election of Assistants.
Admission to Freedom.
The Clerk.   Upon the death of Matthias Fowle the Governor was to be elected Annually. Power was given to the Governor and Assistants to fill up vacancies in their number, and to admit to and make free of the said Company.

Also to choose one honest and discreet person, who shall be called " Clerk of the said Company ;" and Edmund Jeffrey was nominated and appointed First Clerk for life.

Voting.   The Majority of the Assistants, the Governor to be one, were to decide upon all appointments, and business of the Company.

Right of Meeting.   Power was given to the Governor and Assistants to meet together, as often as they might think fit, at their House or Hall, to consult together and to constitute,

Power to make Acts and Ordinances. ordain, and make any Constitutions, Statutes, Laws, Ordinances, Articles, and Orders, which should seem to them reasonable, profitable, or requisite.

Penalties and Fines.   And to inflict all and any such pains, penalties, and punishments, by imprisonment, fine, or amerciament ; and to levy the same by distress or

Recovery of same. otherwise.

Ratification of Acts and Ordinances.   These Laws, Statutes, Articles, etc., were to be engrossed on parchment, and subscribed by the Lord Treasurer, and the Chancellor of the Court of Exchequer.

Beadle.   Power was given to elect one or more Officers, to be called Beadle or Beadles,

His powers and duties. who were to be empowered to take, receive, levy by distress or otherwise, all Fines, Pains, and Penalties, and to execute all the lawful commands and warrants of the Governor and Assistants.

Officers of the Crown to assist the Company.   All Justices, Sheriffs, Mayors, Bailiffs, Constables, and other officers of the Crown, were commanded to be helping, aiding, and assisting the Governor and Assistants.

Prohibition to all not of the Company to engage in the Trade.   All persons not free of the Company were strictly forbidden to engage in this Trade, or import Gold and Silver Thread, etc., etc., upon pain of their wares being forfeited and of the censure and punishment of the Court of Star Chamber.

All Gold and Silver, destined to be used in the said Trade and Manufacture, was first to be brought to the Tower of London, or in default of a convenient room, to the Hall of the Company, there to be prepared and made fit to be sold for the making, working, and drawing of Gold and Silver Wyer. The same was to be prepared according to the fineness of the Standard of His Majesty's coin, with allowance of two-pennyweights for remedy. All metal to be first taken to the Tower, viz. The Mint ; or to the Hall of the Company. Alloying or refining to standard.

The Master, Wardens, and Comptroller of The Mint were enjoined to supervise this operation, and from time to time to take an exact account, and keep a true and just register, as well of all such Gold and Silver as shall have been brought and prepared, as also of all such Bullion and Gold and Silver, as shall have been brought into the Tower of London by the Governor, Assistants, and Commonalty of the Company from foreign parts, there to be converted into current Coin of the Kingdom. Officers of the Mint. Their duties.

The Assay-Master of the Mint, or Assay-Master of the Goldsmiths of the City of London, was charged to make, from time to time, Assays of the fineness and goodness of the Gold and Silver to be prepared in the Tower, or Hall of the Company, for use in the aforesaid Trade. Assay-Masters of the Mint and of the Goldsmiths.

Any person bringing Gold or Silver of a lower quality than the Standard, either to the Tower or Company's Hall, was liable to have one-third part of the same Gold and Silver forfeited to the Crown, and to punishment by the Court of Star Chamber ; or by Fine or imprisonment according to the Statutes, Acts, and Ordinances, which might be provided and made by the Governor and Assistants of the Company. Fines and penalties for having Gold or Silver of quality below the Standard.

Matthias Fowle, the Governor, and his successors, were strictly charged and commanded to survey and oversee the workmanship of the said Gold and Silver wrought and unwrought. Duties of the Governor.

The right of Search, with the assistance of a Constable, and under the Common Seal of the Company, within the City of London, as well as in every other place, within liberties and without, in the Realm of England, and Dominion of Wales, was granted to the Governor, Assistants, and Commonalty. Power was also conferred to board Ships and Vessels, and search for, find, and assay, all base and counterfeit stuff as shall have been imported into, or made and put to sale in the Kingdom ; and if found to be base or counterfeit, to seize and detain the same as forfeited to the Crown. Right of Search. Right to board Vessels.

The Governor for the time being was charged to be diligent and careful in the execution of this duty, and also to give notice and information of all offences and offenders to the Attorney-General, to the end that he might take proceedings in the Court of Star Chamber ; and who was "by these presents" required to prosecute the said offenders accordingly. Information as to offences to be given to the Attorney-General, who was required to prosecute.

The Governor and Assistants, and their successors, were commanded, before putting into execution any of the Grants, Powers, or Authorities hereby given, to take their corporal oath and oaths on the Holy Evangelist before the Master, Warden, and Comptroller of the Mint, within the Tower of London ; who, by this Charter were empowered to administer the same without further warrant. Administration of the Oaths before the High Officers of the Mint.

Joint Bond to be entered into by the Governor and others. The Governor and such of the Assistants as the Lord Treasurer or Chancellor of the Exchequer might select, were required to enter into a joint Bond, under such penalties as the above-mentioned authorities might think fit, for the due performance and observance of the stipulations regarding the importation of Bullion, and its delivery into the Tower.

Separate Bonds of £100 to be given by every member of the Company. The Governor, Assistants, and Commonalty or Freemen of the Company were one and all required to give separate Bonds of One Hundred Pounds each, not to buy or use "other Gould or Silver Wyer" than that to be bought in the Tower of London or Hall of the Company; and also to pay the Duties already specified.

Provision for the custody of the Bonds. The Clerk was authorized to receive these Bonds, which were to be kept by the Company in a chest with two locks, the keys to be held by the Governor and such person who had charge of the Seal wherewith the Gold and Silver Thread had to be sealed.

Rule for the sealing of Gold and Silver Thread, and the payment of Duties. To prevent the manufacture and sale of inferior or unwarrantable Gold and Silver Thread, and for the due informing the Crown of the quantity of Gold and Silver Thread made yearly, the Governor, Assistants, and Commonalty were forbidden to sell any Thread before it had been sealed, and the several Duties, already mentioned, had been paid.

High Officers of the Crown to be aiding and assisting the Company. Finally—The Lord Treasurer, Chancellor, Under Treasurer, the Barons of the Exchequer, and the Attorney-General were charged and enjoined to be aiding and assisting the Governor, Assistants, and Commonalty of the Company.

INDEX.

K

www.ingramcontent.com/pod-product-compliance
Lightning Source LLC
Chambersburg PA
CBHW020551270326
41927CB00006B/797